Theophilus Charles Noble

The Names of those Persons who Subscribe towards the

Defence of this Country at the Time of the Spanish Armada

Theophilus Charles Noble

The Names of those Persons who Subscribe towards the Defence of this Country at the Time of the Spanish Armada

ISBN/EAN: 9783337215996

Printed in Europe, USA, Canada, Australia, Japan

Cover: Foto ©Suzi / pixelio.de

More available books at **www.hansebooks.com**

THE NAMES of those Persons who subscribed towards the Defence of this Country at the time of the SPANISH ARMADA, 1588, and the amounts each contributed.

WITH HISTORICAL INTRODUCTION

BY

T. C. NOBLE; AND INDEX.

London:

ALFRED RUSSELL SMITH,

36, SOHO SQUARE.

1886.

LONDON:

PRINTED BY S. AND J. BRAWN,

GATE STREET, HOLBORN.

INTRODUCTION.

OF the reigns of all the Sovereigns of England, that of Queen Elizabeth is undoubtedly the most momentous. The manners and customs, progresses and pageantry of that half century of English history ; the remarkable men and women who lived in it ; the continuous succession of eventful matters, not only of domestic, but political import, have caused the sovereignty of Elizabeth Tudor to be made the study of all classes of society, historians and critics. And certainly the most noteworthy incident, the most momentous event in the annals of a country, was the invasion of England by the Spanish Fleet in the year of our Lord, 1588. I do not pretend to write at large the history of the Rise and Fall of the Spanish Armada ; but presume to give in as short an essay as possible, so complete a collection of notes upon the subject as could be gathered from the contemporary records of the period, now preserved in various depositories, especially our Public Record Office and the British Museum, where the Burleigh State Papers are to be seen. Yet, notwithstanding the large amount of valuable information we possess, I can but repeat the words of Sir Henry Ellis, the principal Librarian of the British Museum forty years ago—"There are many papers of high historical interest preserved in our manuscript repositories which have not yet seen the light of a later day to explain all

the circumstances attending the formation and defeat of the
Spanish Armada." The discoveries made by Motley, Froude and
other historians of this century prove it ; and, speaking generally,
my own collection of MSS. has from time to time greatly assisted
to settle many a curious genealogical puzzle of the Elizabethan
era.

And here I cannot forbear calling attention to a very curious
fact—the eventful periods in the history of England surrounding
the year '88, from the time of William the Conqueror downwards.
The Domesday Book was finished in A.D. 1086 or 1087, and just
seven hundred years later it was being printed for the first time.
The Conqueror's Charter to the Citizens of London, small as it is
(and still preserved with jealous care by the Corporation) made
all men law-worthy as in King Edward's days, and that each
child should be his father's heir. William the Conqueror died in
September, 1087. A century afterwards Henry Fitzalwyn, citizen
and draper, and ancestor of the Earls of Abingdon, became the
first Mayor (so called) of London, and served in office twenty-
three years. Richard the First was crowned in September 1189,
and both in that year and a century later the poor Jews were
made to suffer terribly for conscience sake. In 1386—8 the ris-
ing of the Lords and the events of the time caused the English
legislature to be called the Merciless Parliament. In August
1485, upon the death of Richard III., the Plantagenet race ended
after a reign of three hundred years. History has fully recorded
the Revolution of 1688 and the abdication of James II., while it
must not be forgotten that the period 1786—93 was a most
momentous one in the annals of the East India Company (founded
soon after the Spanish Armada, in consequence of the riches discovered in the Eastern vessels captured), and that the question
of a Regency through the first attack of insanity suffered by
George III., and his sudden restoration to health made the thanksgiving service at St. Paul's as memorable as that upon the defeat
of the Armada.

In the five years previous to the accession of Queen Elizabeth,
the Roman Catholic religion, during the reign of her Sister Mary

(who married Philip of Spain, the subsequent "hero" of the Armada Plot), had obtained remarkable ascendency. Whether King Philip deserved the Knighthood of the Garter or not, it is not for me to discuss here; but it is worth noting as a very suggestive fact that to this day his Armorial Shield surrounded by the cherished motto is to be seen beautifully painted in the window of the library at Lambeth Palace. From the day of Mary's death, King Philip had remained "a good Catholic," and he was smarting to revenge the persecutions by Henry VIII. and Edward VI. The affairs in the Low Countries, and the depredations on his shipping by the English, under "the flying devil," as Sir Francis Drake was called, the recent execution of Mary Queen of Scots, and the still increasing desire to destroy England's supremacy, and make himself (as he considered he ought to have been) the King of England, and dictator of the world, inspired him to devise the great Armada, which was at one blow to crush for ever the English nation and the Protestant religion. In this truly gigantic scheme he received from that holy man Pope Sextus V. all the assistance possible to be given by promises, blessings and papal bulls. The latter at once settled the matter, for they declared the Invasion no sin; that all men were from henceforth to be absolved from their oath of allegiance to the Queen of England, and that he who first took possession of our Island was to be the rightful occupier of the throne : that man of course was to be King Philip himself.

Queen Elizabeth however was a very different person to what Philip would have us believe. She was not going to give up the snug little island so easily. Previous to the Armada year she had received for some time much information relating to mysterious proceedings abroad, and though she affected to pay no attention, there is no doubt she thought a very great deal upon the subject. In May 1582 a Scottish Jesuit had been arrested, upon whom was found a paper written in Italian, referring to a proposed Invasion and the deposition of the Queen, and there is still preserved among the state papers* the Attorney General's own notes

* S. P. Domestic Series, Eliz., Vol. 153, No. 79.

of the proposed Invasion, 1583. Then again Sir George Carey, the Governor of the Isle of Wight, wrote to Sir Francis Walsingham, the Secretary of State,[*] on the 30th January, 1583 (4) that he had received good advice from one Jacob Whiddon, the master of a ship just returned from Lisbon, a man "seeminge to be bothe sober, discrete and of reasonable judgement," that "greate pparation be in hande for arminge a navie this sommer to the Sea ffive gallies to be upon the Stockes whereof one excedethe in bignes anie heretofore made by the halfe," and "that the Kinge determinethe in psonne to go this intended voyage wth an armie of manye thousandes of menne," the designe being "to accomplishe some acceptable service to God for Subv^{r}sion of religion in England, and that the plott was laid that all his Biscayens should lande at Milforde; the Kinge about Southchampton; the French Kinge at that instant to proclaime warre against us and to enter by Scotlande ioyninge with the Scottish forces to invade us." Sir George Carey concludes by begging that the information be received with secrecy, for if such "soddenne exploicte shoulde happenne I have not foure greate peeces mounted ne^r a forte or platteforme in state serviceable no^r goode powlder to mainteine shotte for one daies service," adding by way of sarcastic remark "Yf this place be of so smale importannce to be thought worthie of no better provision."

Now this letter is of the greatest historical importance, for it proves generally what really did take place four years afterwards —the actual invasion of England by an army of many thousands of men. The letter is dated from Carisbrooke Castle, in which (it will be remembered) sixty-four years afterwards Charles the First, King of England was himself a prisoner, and if coincidences are worth anything, the letter is dated the fatal 30th of January, upon which day sixty-five years later (1648—9) that misled monarch was beheaded at Whitehall!

Among the Records are preserved no less than twelve pages of the examination of four Spaniards in June 1585, to whom a

[*] S. P. dom. 167 (53).

dozen questions were put as to Philip's designs; and some six months later Lord Burghley sent to Walsingham certain details, among which was a charge upon ecclesiastics (Bishops, &c.) for the provision of Light Horse and Lancers, which he reckoned at £25 each, bringing a total of £8,275. This is interesting, showing that the Clergy were not exempt, and in 1588 they provided 559 horsemen and 3885 foot. In December 1585 one Walker Squior just returned from Lisbon to Dartmouth speaks of eighty sail of Hulks, of from 100 to 800 tons each; twenty Galleons of 300 to 500 tons; forty Biscay ships of 100 to 500 tons; with 30,000 Germans, 20,000 Italians (to be provided by the Pope), 5,000 Spaniards, and 7,000 Portuguese, all them getting ready for the Invasion of England.* Now this information was considered but an exaggerated idea of Philip's plans; however in March following there is the important correspondence of one Walsingham's agents, Thomas Rogers (Nicholas Berden) which it is said formed the basis of England's future action. Among the proposals it was stated that if King Philip lent 10,000 crowns to the Duke of Guise, the latter would arm 800 French Footte and 200 horses, and that he would take the port of Weymouth, and keep it for his (Philip's) use.† A few months later, in a letter dated from Exeter, 14th December, 1586, Sir John Gilberte writes to Walsingham, that he has heard upon good authority that the King of Spain is preparing a fleet of ships with 60,000 soldiers " too have hys revenge apone Ingelande.‡

With such evidence it is therefore quite clear that Philip had secretly, and for a long time previous to the actual invasion, made every preparation, and that all the resources of Spain, assisted by Portugal, Italy and Naples, were to be brought into use for the grand attack upon the little island of England. Of course Philip knew the characteristics of the English people. While he was thus preparing to crush us he proposed a conference, with a

* S. P. Dom. 185 (16).

† S. P. Dom. 187 (81).

‡ Harl. MS. 295 (Brit. Mus.) fo. 178.

view of settlement of all disputes, in the Netherlands, and Queen
Elizabeth either believed him, or feigned to do so; for such a conference took place between the two countries, and it may be said
that both sides knew it was only that each might gain sufficient
extra time to bring about more surely the Invasion and the defeat.
Did we not know from other evidences the peculiarities of the
Queen, and her extraordinary niggardness even in the hour of the
greatest danger, we should be much inclined to wonder at a pro-
ceeding which might have brought about the wreck of her ships,
the ruin of her fortresses, and the starvation of all her brave men.
Subsequent events proved that had it not been for better
generals than she — notwithstanding that she took upon herself the whole management, the book-keeping and counting-
house work of this ever to be remembered and really leviathan
defence of England, showing her to have been a woman of no
ordinary character;—had it not been for the Lord Admiral
Howard, for Drake and Raleigh, harassing from time to time the
Spaniards even against the Queen's orders, there is every reason
to believe that the Invasion would have taken place long before
England was ready to defend herself.

In May, 1586, Drake had given "a cooling" to King Philip, by
capturing 20 Spanish ships, with 250 brass pieces,[*] and in April,
1587, he tells us in a letter[†] still preserved, that at Calais on the
19th, "fynding divers huge shippes loden and to be loden with
the King's provision for England," he in his quiet business like
way "burnt xxxij and sanke a greate argosie, and carried awaie
fower w'th us"—sank two of the King's galleys, and repulsed the
remainder "with verie little losse on our ptie," notwithstanding the
heavy fire from the shore. The preparations of the King were
greater than ever heard of before. Having "singed the King of
Spain's beard" he braved Santa Cruz, the Spanish Admiral, to
come out and fight, a challenge not readily accepted, for if any
man had created a terror, both by sea and land, it was our Devon-

---

[*] S. P. dom. 189 (23).

[†] Ibid. 200 (47).

shire Drake, and the most remarkable part is that we have no record that all these exploits were done "by order"—in fact, it is believed to have been the reverse, for our official documents sadly prove the miserable condition our navy was in. It is certainly worth noting that in one of his captures (says Camden), of "a great and lusty ship, most rich and well furnished, called Saint Phillip, which was returning from the East Indies,"—the wealth found upon it gave a hint to the English which a few years later (in 1600), gave rise to the East India Company. Lord Burghley was continually lamenting, in his letters to Walsingham and in one dated Sept. 13, 1587 (even when the Armada would have been at our door, had not a mightier power than the Queen of England decreed otherwise), he speaks of the decay of the ships, the arrears of pay due to the men, and the troops a quarter of their real strength.

From the Court at Richmond, 10th October, 1587, Burghley wrote to the Deputy Lieutenants of the Counties, informing them of "the great preparations now partlie made readie in Spaine for the furniture of a mightie armie with a nauie to come partilie to the seas," and desiring that all the musters should be in full strength and prepared; in November they were directed to have in readiness 20,000 footmen, 3,000 horsemen, and 1,000 pioneers, "for hir majties person;" and in January, Kent certified that that County was prepared with at least 12,654 men and 1,000 more from the Cinque ports. This proves how patriotic the people were at the hour of danger.

King Philip in the meantime had made all arrangements to sail. It is true there was already discontent in his forces at delay, while abroad—in Paris—one writer adds: "The Pope's signe hath brought into this country such sickness and dearth that I think the Kinge and all wishe him hanged." It was a misfortune to Philip that, just on the eve of sailing, his admiral Santa Cruz died, and the weather became very bad. Drake too had certainly weakened him, so that the Invasion promised in September or January was compelled to be postponed. Had not these circumstances intervened, not even the well known pluck of "a true born Englishman," would, I think, have saved England. This may be said to be theory, but our original records too truly prove that we were no more fit to meet an enemy then, or even three months later, thus making the history of this descent upon England more memorable than may be, at first supposed. And the great blame rested not on British valour, or the want of funds, but really on the Queen herself. I have in my own collection of MSS. a document illustrative of the period of the threatened invasion a few years later than that of the Armada. In it stores of immediate necessity to the amount of £1500 are shewn to have been cut down to just £760! Mr. Froude, severe as he is, only tells that truth which, until this century dawned, was an unknown virtue with the historians of the Spanish Armada.

Some of the ships of the period had worn well. There was Drake's "Fortunate Ship," the Elizabeth Bonaventure, which after 27 years' hard work, had run aground in March, 1587 (8), but still was unimpaired, causing the Lord Admiral to remark "except a ship had bene made of iron it were to be thought impossible to do as she hath done," an expression more of its capital build than the term iron, for now-a-days, our iron vessels instead of floating and lasting, turn up their toes suddenly and sink to the bottom of the sea, which "the wooden walls" of old England never did. What would Queen Elizabeth have thought of our ships now, when she considered hers to be expensive toys? Her Lord Admiral was clamouring, begging, praying, for the means of defence—ships, ammunition and provisions. "For the love of Jesus Christ, madam, awake," wrote he to her on the 2nd June, 1588. No wonder Froude writes: "She skipped, and joked, and wrangled over her money bags as if the Spanish Fleet was a dream and Philip fabulous as a wizard of romance." And when she did awake for a brief space, she simply allowed out a month's supply of stores—in fact, the brave men who were really risking their lives for England, were living at the rate of six men partaking of provisions only sufficient for four; sour beer and no ammunition to depend upon. The Lord Admiral himself actually paid out of his own pocket for the necessaries of existence for his men, because it was too much trouble for the Queen to write an order for them to be given out at the Tower. But history repeats itself, and our own Crimean experience shows how hard it is to learn wisdom.

Such was the state of affairs when the great and " Invincible Armada " was not only approaching, but actually in sight of England. Even Scotland, which probably, might be expected to have proved troublesome to us, seeing that Elizabeth had beheaded King James's mother only a few months previously, at last moved on the defensive. At a council in Holyrood House, May 7th, 1588, the king was informed* " how utheris Princes and potentates in Europe haue putt thameselffs in armes within their kingdomes and dominions, having in reddynes grite and mychtic armeis preparit for sum grite purpois and exployte," whereupon it was proclaimed that all men between the ages of 16 and 60 were to be prepared at six hours warning to " ryse and marche," and other directions were issued in readiness for the defence of Scotland.

The magnitude of the Armada did not decrease by the intelligence of the day. In March, Howard wrote to Walsingham that the Spanish Fleet consisted of 210 sail and 36,000 soldiers; in May, Lord Seymour reported it to be 300 sail; next it was 130 sail of 57,868 tons burthen, 30,655 men, 2,080 galley slaves, 90 hangmen or executioners, 19 justices, and 2,360 pieces of ordnance. Then 132 sail of 59,120 tons burthen, 29,621 soldiers, 2,088 slaves, and finally, another report was 160 sail and 36,000 men. But probably, the correct estimate was 166 ships (all told), 27,128 Castilian and Portuguese soldiers, marines, and pioneers, and 180 friars. The flower of the nobility of the country were represented in the expedition. The King, in the place of Santa Cruz, who died, appointed the Duke of Medina Sidonia, Lord Admiral, and his correct title (Englished), is worth repeating, as some writers have mistaken another Duke Medina, for him : " Don Alonso Peres de Gusman, the Good Duke of the City of Medina Sidonia, Earl of Niobla, Marquis of Cacaca, in Africa, Lord of the City of St. Lucars, Captain General of the

* Reg. Privy Council Scot. IV.

Ocean Sea, and the Coast of Andalusia, and the Riall Army and Host of His Majesty, and Knight of the famous order of the Golden Fleece." The orders he issued dated the 22nd May, 1588, and forty in number, are very curious and worthy of study, the first being the object of the invasion : " to serve God our Lord, and to bring again to his church and bosom many people and souls, which being oppressed by the hereticks and enemies of our Holy Catholick faith, they keep in subjection into their sects and unhappiness." *

With the expedition was brought a supply of provisions for six months, including biscuits, fish, rice, cocoa, wine, water, oil, candles, vinegar, etc. ; in fact, Drake estimated the quantity sufficent to keep 40,000 men a year. Twelve of the largest ships were named after the twelve apostles, a religious pass-word was given for each day of the week, and upon the standards were painted figures of Jesus Christ, our Lady, and the King of Spain.

To meet this force, the English fleet consisted of 195 ships (all told), and 15,334 men, of which only 61 ships and 7,901 men were in the direct pay of the Government for the month ending 25th August, 1588, being within the actual period of "Armada Service." The fleet was divided into three squadrons, under the command of Charles Howard, Baron of Effingham (afterwards created, in 1596, the first Earl of Nottingham, and High Steward of England, at the Coronation of James the First) as Lord High Admiral ; Lord Henry Seymour ; and Sir Francis Drake. But, large as the force appears, it really represented but half of war-ship standard. The majority were vessels supplied by various ports and places in England, to contribute which was in many instances a great hardship. The Governor of the Isle of Wight, declared there was no vessel belonging to that Island over 20 tons burthen, and Southampton, through the decay of the town and commerce, could not provide the two ships and pinnace asked for, and even if it could, it had not the men, for 110 had already been pressed in that place. Ipswich

* These "orders" will be found printed in the Harleian Miscellany, Vol. i., p. 115 ; Somer's State Tracts, Vol. i., p. 425; Jour. Arch. Association, Vol. ix., p. 332.

and Harwich would provide the two ships and pinnace, but desired
the Government to provide the ordnance ; Exeter, informing the
Lord Treasurer of the ships being ready, state their cost to that ·
city to be £1,000.   The Cinque Ports fitted out six ships of 160
tons each, and six pinnaces of 30 tons, to attend upon them, " and
among other service performed against the enemy, one of their
ships, of Dover, the marines of which were well acquainted with the
flats and banks of the Channel, decoyed the great Galleas of Spain
and run her aground on the coast near Calais, and afterwards
burnt her."*

The Lord Admiral's ship, "The Ark," carried 425 men ;
Lord   Seymour's   was   "The   Rainbow,"   and   Sir   Francis
Drake's "The Revenge," each with 250 men.   Among the
other ships of the fleet were " The Triumph " (Sir Martin Frobis-
her, with 150 men)—"The Victory" (Sir John Hawkins, 400)—
" The Lyon " (Lord Thomas Howard, 250)—"The Bonaventure"
(Earl of Cumberland, 250,)—"The Dreadnought " (Sir George Bes-
ton, 200)—"The Vantguard " (Sir William Winter, 500).   Among
the merchant ships were the " Gallian Leycester " (George Fenner,
160)—"The Golden Noble " (Adam Seiger, 110)—"The Thomas
Drake," and "The Elizabeth Drake," " The Hope Hawkins," " The
Diamond," " The Heart's Ease," and " The Virgin, God save her."
Among the London ships were " The Hercules," " The Royal Defence," "The Centurion," "The George Noble," " The Providence,"
and, what will please our American cousins, "The Mayflower " (of
200 tons, with 90 men, Captain Edward Banke), which was also
the name of one of the coasters sent from King's Lynn, in Norfolk
(150 tons, 70 men, Capt. Alexander Musgrave).   Some of the other
names are curious, for there was " The Foresight," " The
Swiftsure," " The Hopewell," " The Delight," " The Makeshift,"
" The Bark Buggans," " The Gift of God," " The Vyneyard," " The
Handmaid," " The Little Hare," " The Grace of God," " The Sly-
boot," and " The Heathen of Weymouth."

The land force was equally a weighty matter.   Like the navy, the

* Hasted's Hist. of Kent, Vol. iv., p. 79.

army had been quite a secondary consideration. The General Commander-in-Chief was the Queen's favourite, the Earl of Leicester, of whom Froude speaks:—"Drake's ability was as conspicuous as Leicester's imbecility," and it must be acknowledged that the Earl's ability had been proved wanting in the Netherlands. The English musters were ordered to be reported upon as early as 1584, and it may be a fact of some interest to note that Thomas Churchyard, the poet, was Muster Master for the County of Kent. The reports subsequently collected, shew there were 87,281 men in England, and 45,408 in Wales; in all, 132,689. This body was divided into three divisions, which specially included 22,000 foot and 2,000 horse, for the defence of London, under Leicester, at Tilbury; 28,900 under Lord Hunsdon; and 27,000 foot and 407 lances horse, and 1,961 light horse, as a reserve. Thus stood the force in June, 1588. On the 27th of that month 1,800 men were called out of Surrey. The Canterbury City records* give most interesting details of the Kentish preparations, and of the Camp at Northborne, near Deal. From that city went especially equipped, Alderman Brome at the head of 200 men; his namesake had done a similar service for Edward the Fourth, in 1470. We are told by Mr. Sheppard† that the repeated charges in the City accounts for "new heddyng of a drumme" shew but too wel the zeal displayed in beating to arms. In Sussex enthusiasm was equally strong. One incident is worth recording: the old and infirm Viscount Montague collected together 200 horse, and marched at the head of them with his sons and child grandson, to offer his services to the Queen at Tilbury.‡ No wonder Her Majesty "finding him faithful, always loved him,"—although it must be acknowledged in a great many instances, Elizabeth proved herself forgetful of those who served her. In Norfolk, from May to September, 1588, the total cost for preparations amounted to £4,241, of which £2,272 was spent on 3,000 soldiers "appoynted for her Majties guard to

* Hist. MSS., ix. 158.
† Arch. Cant., xii., 42.
‡ Sussex, Arch. Coll., vii., 181.

martch towards London."* The Lewes town books record that 42 barrels of gunpowder, 120 shot, 6 pieces of ordnance, match, etc., were delivered to that place, "of whiche 42 barrels of gunne powder there were delyuered unto the use of the Right Hon. Lord Buckhurste, 20 at the time that the Spanishe fleete came along by Newe Haven for my Lord Admirall; and also one other barrell of the same 42 barrells of Gunpowder, was by a warrant directed unto the said constables from the Lord Buckhurste delyuered unto one, Patrick Hackett, for the use of the town of Brithhelmston." (Brighton).†

London naturally was fully alive to the danger from the earliest moment. The citizens from the most ancient times have always proved the best guardians of the Monarch and the People. And when the crown has failed in its duty, the loyal inhabitants who have been contemptuously called, by evil and jealous outsiders, "the shopkeepers of one square mile," have come forward and proved themselves ready to defend the rights and privileges of a great nation. "The firmly rooted tree of the British Constitution, beneath whose spacious branches repose and safety are now possible, was planted and watched and nurtured, by bold true Englishmen of former days. Personal, civil, and religious freedom, commercial greatness, social prosperity, cultivated intelligence, far-reaching philanthropy, vast moral influence, are the product of seeds planted long ago, and whose growth a benign Providence has fostered."‡ When therefore the Lords of the Council, in June, 1588, demanded of the citizens 10,000 men, the demand was immediately complied with. The Lord Mayor, further, called upon the City Companies, and the members put down their names for £54,000. The "Twelve" great Livery Guilds (among 219 members) alone subscribed £43,700, and among these the Ironmongers', to which I have the honour to belong, put down their names for £2,300. On the 3rd of April, the Corporation of London had resolved to fit out 16 of the

* Lausdowne MS., 58, (156.)

† Horsfield's Hist. Sussex, i., 123.

‡ 'London's Roll of Fame,' 1884 (32).

largest ships and 4 pinnaces, and in July, it was reported that these 20 vessels (with 2,140 men), were costing the citizens £2,291 per month, yet they were willing to victual them one month longer. By that date we know the defeat of the Armada had been accomplished. Then again the Churchwardens' accounts of the different parishes in England give some interesting records. In London, those of St. Dunstan, Fleet Street, tells us, " Item paid for Papr, Einke, and Pennes, when the Alderman came to sesse men for armour, vd. Item paid for Gunpowder, xijd." St. Margaret's, Westminster, shew that parish particularly active in scouring its corslets and sharpening its steel ; " payd at the mustering in Tutill fields, the xxj Aprill, for Powder, xxjlb., xxjs," and for 5 lbs of Match 20d." And what is particularly noteworthy : " for twoe prayere bookes when the Spanish fleete was upon the narrowe seas, iijd." Those interested in " The Marshalling of the Citie of London into a true forme of discipline," may see in the report of Edmunde Yorke, a commander in the Low Countries, many curious details.*

This tract on the marshalling, reminds us that the history of the trained bands of Old England forms a very interesting chapter in the annals of the country. The Honourable Artillery Company of the City of London was then, as now is, a force composed of citizens, " good and true," and we are told that many of the officers of the ancient corps were, at the time of the Armada, chosen to command in other parts of the kingdom, and that it was through their care and attention the trained bands in the provinces were so marshalled as to be a credit to the nation.† In the regiments from the counties sent to London, were many representatives of the first families in England, and of those who marched towards Tilbury was one man who was a namesake and one of the family of the future Lord Protector. This Oliver Cromwell, one of the Captains of the Huntingdon 400, was, it is true, not *the* General who, half a

---

* Lansdowne, MS., 56 (35) printed in Strype's Stowe's " Survey of London," and " Antiquarian Repertory."

† Raike's Hist. Hon. Artill. Co., Vol. i., p. 34.

century later, was to make all England tremble (for the Protector was not born until 1599), but it is curious, never the less, that one of the name should be among the first to take up arms against Spain, in defence of our rights and privileges.

At last, on the 19th (29th N. S.), May, 1588, 129 vessels, carrying 19,295 soldiers, and 8,460 sailors, with slaves, and all other necessary belongings to the Spanish fleet, together with 2,431 pieces of ordnance, sailed gaily from Lisbon on its vaunted mission of Christianity (?) The Prince of Parma had promised to join the Invincibles with 35,000 men, but unfortunately for Spain, there was, from first to last, a Power greater than man who controlled matters, and this Power made itself felt in a very significant way. The Spanish Admiral was not used to the work he was appointed to oversee, the Prince of Parma did not, or could not, see his way clear to appear, while the wind and weather became so boisterous that the poor fleet suffered so severely as to be forced into the Groyne for repairs, and this causing a further delay of several weeks, prevented the Armada from reaching England at the time when England was not prepared to defend itself. We cannot get rid of such facts as original documents proclaim, and, I repeat, England had to thank a greater Power than the Queen for its preservation.

It was on the 12th (22) of July, that the Spaniards again sailed, and a week later the Armada was in the English Channel. Howard, Drake, and the others of our fleet, had been anxiously watching for the strangers. At last, says Camden, "they discovered the Spanish fleet, with lofty turret-like castles in front, like a half moon, the wings thereof spreading out about the length of seven miles, sailing very slowly with full sails, the wind being, as it were, overid with carrying them, and the ocean groaning under their weight." The Lords of the Council had written to the County Lieutenants that all troops under command should "be in readiness upon the fyeringe of the Beacons" to defend, and when the firing did take place, such a blaze along the English coast had never been seen before. "Myselfe can remember," writes an eye-witness, "when, upon the fyrcing of the Beacons (whereby an alarum was given), the country people, forthwith, ranne downe to the seaside,

b

some with clubs, some with picked staves and pitchforkes, all un-armed, and they that were best appoynted were but with a bill, a bow, and a sheafe of arrowes, no captaine or commander appoynted to direct, lead, or order them."* This explains the enthusiasm of the people, and it also truly shews "how dangerous it weare by tarrying to arme and put men in order, whereby their heat and fury might wax colde;" the old principle of defence. The general call to arms had sounded, and the troops marched towards the coast with a spirit "eager for the fray." Another eye-witness, no less a personage than John Stow, the honest historian of our London City, tells us:—"It was a pleasant sight to beholde the soldiers as they marched towards Tilbury, their cheerfull countenances, courageous words and gestures, dauncing and leaping, wheresoever they came, and in the campe their moste felicitie was hope of fight with y⁰ enemye."† Leicester, himself, wrote to Walsingham :—"the 4,000 men are all com together and lodged here, at West Tylberry . . . . . they be as forward men, and all wyllying to mete w^t the enemye as ever I saw," but their sudden call had prevented them bringing provisions, so that they were in a terrible plight—"there was not a barrell of bere nor a lofe of bredd for them after xx myles march." Such was the way we looked after our troops 300 years ago. And a proclamation actually had to be issued, limiting the prices of provisions,‡ for, as the demand increased, so increased the price ! No wonder even Leicester wondered that the soldiers were not more discouraged, and that he stopped 1,000 more men coming from London, unless they brought with them their rations. It was something for Leicester to do, to beg that the kingdom might not be played away by delay, but this he really did.

Across the river Thames from Tilbury Fort to Gravesend, was thrown a chain and a bridge of boats, to prevent a passage up the river by the enemy, and to provide communication between Kent and Essex, for our troops. And here is another fact worth record-

* Harl. MSS., 132 and 4685 ; and Dulwich Coll. MSS., xxix.
† Annals, 1615, p. 742.
‡ Copy in Soc. Antiq. Coll., Vol. v., 262.

ing. Peter Pett, the Engineer, had an interview with Leicester about completing this very bridge, on the 22nd July, three days *after* the Armada had been seen in the Channel! A chart shewing the Thames between Lambeth and Tilbury Hope, is to be found in Robert Adam's 'Expeditionis Hispanorum in Angliam vera Descriptio,' 1588, a work which suggested those famous tapestries formerly in the House of Lords, and unfortunately destroyed when the Parliament Houses were burnt. These tapestries had been designed by Henry Cornelius Vroom, and executed by Francis Spering. In 1739 the Rev. Philip Morant, the Essex historian, described, and Pine illustrated, in an elegant folio volume, the ten pieces; in the preface to which is the foreboding, now of melancholy value : "as accident or moths may deface these valuable shadows, we have endeavoured to preserve their likeness in the preceding prints."

To this valuable record, to Froude, Motley and others of our modern historians who have carefully digested the State Papers, a reference must be made for a history of the fighting, and all the exciting incidents attending it. Suffice to say here that on the 21st (31) July the Lord Admiral had proclaimed war from his pinnace "The Defiance ;" that Sir Francis Drake gave " a slap in the face " to the enemy, by not only taking a Spanish Galleon with all on board, including something like 50,000 ducats, but had actually captured Don Pedro de Valdez himself, " a man of great estimation with the King of Spayne, and thought next in his army to the Duke of Sidonia ; " that fighting lasted on the 23rd July (August 2nd) from morning till night, when, says Camden, " there was never more lightening and thundering of the artillery than there was on both sides," and yet only one man was killed, on the side of the English, and he died " glorious " in his own barque in the midst of the enemy. The sharpest engagement took place on the 25th (August 4) in view of the Isle of Wight ; the next day the Spaniards sailed up channel, hoping to meet Parma and his promised aid, but Lord Henry Seymour had already taken up a position to prevent Parma leaving his own country ; and a few hours later the enemy anchored off Calais.

It was here in the darkness of the night, the English stratagem, which brought about the thorough rout of the Armada, was carried into effect. Some old and useless hulks were filled with inflammables, and being towed and drifted silently among the Spanish ships were suddenly fired. The result may be easily guessed; a panic ensued, orders to cut cables were sounded, and on the 28th July (August 7) out of 124 ships then anchored, only 86 could the next day be found,* the rest had vanished in different directions in dismay. Although not a new idea, this stratagem was certainly one of the best tactics adopted throughout the whole period of the Invasion, for during the excitement the English took the opportunity of "settling" one of the largest galleasses, in which its Commander Hugh de Moncado with 400 of his men perished, and 300 slaves jumping overboard were liberated; this was on the 29th July (August 8). The Spaniards, followed by the English, steered along the coast of Flanders, but the wrecks needed little following; their work was done; wind and weather were to do the rest.

Sir John Hawkins writing from on board the Victory, July 31st (August 10) gives us a summary of the fight: "Our ships, God be thanked, have received littell hurte," and that tells a remarkable tale. Sir John complains that the men of our fleet "have been long unpaid and need releefe." Drake wrote the same day to Walsingham: "There was never anything pleased me better than the seeing the enemy flying with a south wind to the northwards. God grant they have a good eye to the Duke of Parma, for with the grace of God, if we live, I doubt it not, but ere it be long so to handle the matter with the Duke of Sidonia as he shall wish himself at Saint Marie among his orange trees."† And Sir William Wynter writing the next day, August 1st (11), after declaring that their victuals on board ship were at an end, remarks, "the Duke would give his dukedom to be in Spain again!" That day, the Commanders of the English Fleet held a

* S. P. Dom. 213 (67).

† S. P. Dom. 213 (73).

council, and they (the Lord Admiral Howard; George Clifford, third Earl of Cumberland; Lord Thomas Howard; Sir Francis Drake: Edmond, third Lord Sheffield; Sir John Hawkins; Sir Edward Hoby; and Vice Admiral Thomas Fenner) then and there declared their determination "to folowe and pursue the Spanishe fleete untill we have cleared our owne coaste and brought the Frithe west of us. And then to returne backe againe as well to revictuall oure ships (which stand in extreame scarcitie) as alsoe to guard and defende oure owne coaste at home, with furthor protestatione that if oure wantes of victualles and munitione were supplied we wold pursue them to the furthest."* This document is not only of interest, but important, for it proves how sadly deficient the fleet was in stores and provisions.

While all this was going on aboard ship, the army on land was mustering and marching towards the coast. On the 24th July (August 3) Leicester received his commission in command at Tilbury, and three days later he wrote to the Queen, proposing, that she on her way to Havering, should spend two or three days in "yor pore Lyvetenants Cabin," resting at Mr. Thomas Rich's house at Horndon, and so "make gladd many thousandes both here and not farr off." Accordingly on the 5th (15th) August, Her Majesty (not forgetting the princely pleasures of Kenilworth in 1575) once more favored her favourite, and as history tells us passed through the lines of troops at Tilbury on a white palfrey, addressing the soldiers with a true martial spirit. Here she dined with, and smiled upon those around her, and promised, no doubt, many a reward she soon forgot to bestow. Sir Edward Ratcliffe was one, and it was he who when subsequently jokingly asked by the Queen what a man thought of when thinking of nothing, replied with all humility : " Madam, he thinks of a woman's promise !" To Tilbury came Robert Carey and the Earl of Cumberland, to bring the Queen news of the Armada's defeat, so that it is a remarkable fact, illustrative of the times and the general order of things, that at the very time Her Majesty was addressing the troops, and cheering them on to victory, the Invincible

* Grenville MS., Brit. Mus.

Armada had been defeated at least a week, not one hundred miles from where she was, and some of the English vessels had already returned home !

The fate of the Armada is recorded in history. On St. Lawrence's day July 30th (August 9), Philip the Second was destined to know the Saints had deserted his cause, notwithstanding the blessings of the Pope. And still more curious is it to record that in all the fighting, while amunition and provisions had been expended on both sides, until each fleet had not sufficient powder to fight another day,* yet Providence ruled the destinies of each, as to bring about a cessation at so opportune a moment, that while at least 10,000 men had been killed on the Spanish side, not one hundred Englishmen had been slain. When Howard left the enemy going north there were, or should have been, at least 120 sail. Sir George Carey on the 22nd August (September 1) reports one hundred big vessels then steering between the Orkneys and Fair Island, beat about by the winds; but a fortnight later only fifty-two of these had escaped destruction through the weather, winds and rocks. In the fighting of July and August fifteen ships and 4,791 men were reported lost ; in September on the coast of Ireland seventeen ships and 5,394 men perished by the tempest,† so that if these returns are correct, thirty-two ships and 10,185 men perished in this expedition. Of seventy other ships nothing more was heard ; one of the largest galleons on the Irish coast begged for water, although it had twenty-five pipes of wine on board. "Our Lady of the Rosary," a fine ship with 700 hands, had lost 500 : and those that survived in great want, were Spanish gentry born ; but soon afterwards the vessel struck the breakers of the Blasket Island, and the pilot's son alone was saved. In another case, a butt of wine was offered for a cask of water, and that not being obtained, even the ship itself ; but the Irish were too much afraid of the gallows to accept the tempting bait, and so the vessel foundered, and of the

---

* Memoirs of Carey, p. 17—22.

† Carew MS. 611 (149).

crew, all that survived were taken prisoners. Two other big ships were seen off the Isle of Arran, but one of these suddenly disappeared, and the other became a prize for the Mayor of Galway. The remnants of the proud Armada in passing round by Scotland presented a most dismal spectacle. On the strand at Sligo, wrote Secretary Fenton to Lord Burleigh, October 28th, there were to be seen in a five-mile walk 1,100 dead bodies washed up by the sea.* Of the officers wrecked Don Lewis of Cordova alone escaped, being sent to England. It was long reported, even believed to this day by the residents, that the great Duke of Medina himself had been wrecked on the Fair Island,† and was never more seen in Spain; but this was really only a superstition, for both Mr. Froude and Mr. Motley have proved by the Spanish records that the Duke had returned home in September 1588, and soon retired a disgraced and disgusted man to his own quiet estate.

But the foundering of so many Spanish vessels with the fabulous treasures on board, led to much speculation in after years. Between 1641 and 1694 the records of the Argyll family‡ shew that the Marquis had obtained a grant from Charles I. to search for the "Admiral of Florence" ship of fifty-six guns with thirty millions of money on board, wrecked on the coast of Mull, but in 1677 after a long search, all that was found were a few odd things, such as kettles, &c., and copper just sufficient to pay the cost of the search! This reminds me of a more modern venture. In 1869 a limited liability Company was started in London, with a capital of £100,000, to recover the vast treasures from the Galleons sunk in the Harbour of Vigo in the Spanish War of Succession, 1700, and supposed to contain fourteen millions of Eights. In 1873 the expedition returned to Havre, the apparatus, cranes, &c., on board comprising, I understand, the sole assets of the company.

When the news of the defeat of the Armada reached Rome, the wits spared not the actors in it. An unofficial proclamation was

* S. P. Dom. 216.
† See Notes and Queries, 4th Ser.
‡ Hist. MS., VI.

issued in these words :—"The Pope from the plenitude of his power will grant indulgences for 1000 years, if any one will inform him with certainty what is become of the Spanish Fleet; where it is gone; whether it be taken up to Heaven; sunk down into Tartarus; suspended somewhere in the air; or floating upon some sea." Lord Bacon, in 1624, did not fail to ridicule it, and at the present day the only relics we have of the Invincibles and their treasures are the "curiosities" in the Tower of London—the lances which were brought over "to bleed us with;" the peculiar instrument called the Ranceur, in which is a pike intended "to pick the roast beef out of the Englishman's teeth;" the collar of torment; and a few other similar pretty little toys which were intended to amuse and convert us.

The defeat of the Armada was the subject of no end of literature, as the Register Books at Stationer's Hall duly chronicle. Songs, ballads, psalms, and verses were the order of the day. There was one curious sheet printed off in various languages, a copy of which is still preserved among the Cottonian MS.* But perhaps the most curious is the "long and crafty" letter of thirty leaves, which Lord Burghley addressed to the Spanish Ambassador in France, in which he detailed, in the assumed character of a papist in England, the lamentable defeat.† Then again pictures and medals appeared to suit the people and the times; subsequently illustrated Armada playing cards were invented "to keep the memory green,"‡ and such entries were made in the parish registers, as may be seen in those at Carisbrooke, in the Isle of Wight. Then again paintings were introduced; as those in Gaywood Church, Norfolk; All Saints', Hastings; and Beddington Hall;§ but probably the most interesting memorial is that in St. Helen's Church, Bishopsgate, in the City of London—it is a monument erected to the memory of Martin Bond, the son of

* Titus, B VIII. (351).
† Lansdowne MS., 55 (134).
‡ Arch. Jour. XI. (180).
§ N. & Q., 1st ser., vii. 558.; Suss. Arch. Coll. xxiii. 194.

the celebrated Alderman Bond, so well known for his Eastern trading ships, and one of the Royal Commissioners. The inscription tells us that Martin Bond " was Captaine in ye yeare 1588 at ye campe at Tilbury, and after remained Chief Captaine of ye trained bands of this Citty untill his death,"—in 1643, aged 85. He was a member of the Haberdashers' Company, who recently restored the monument, which curiously represents the Captain seated in a tent at the camp; two sentinels are in front, and at the side is a page holding a horse, while in the rear are other tents. To this day in various places in England, sermons are annually preached by virtue of bequests left for the special purpose " of expressing thankfulness to God for his mercifull deliverance of this kingdom in the year of our lord God 1588 from the Spanish Armada," and also deliverance from the Gunpowder Plot Conspirators of 1605.*

The Public Thanksgiving at St. Paul's must not be forgotten. Her Majesty surrounded by her Court proceeded in state from Somerset House in the Strand, through Temple Bar,† over the gates of which were placed the City Waits, and at the entrance stood the Lord Mayor with the Sceptre, which he presented to the Queen, and she returned it to him as she considered it could not be in better custody, and so through lines of the trained bands and the Livery of London to the Cathedral. This was on the 24th November, 1588, when the Bishop of Sarum preached from Paul's Cross, then standing at the north-east corner of the present cathedral. The books of the various City Companies show the great preparations made upon the occasion. The Stationers' (Francis Coldocke and Henry Denham, being then Wardens) not only record the repair of the pavements at the West end of the Church, but also " for preparacōn of standinge and for fflaggies and other necessaryes," as also " for twoo severall dynners,"‡

* Chapman 1616 and 1626, St. Mary-le-Bow, Cheapside.—Wilcox 1627, Alcester.—Jackson 1630, Nottingham.—Hayne 1640, Leicester.

† See my ' Memorials of Temple Bar with some account of Fleet Street,' 1869.

‡ Arber's Registers of the Stationer's Company.

showing what a time of festivity it was. The Churchwardens'
books of the various parishes likewise recorded the ringing of the
bells, and refreshment to the ringers. At St. Margaret's Westminster, two shillings were paid (which was twelve pence more than
was "payde for ringinge at the beheadinge of the Quene of Scots,"
although the very next entry in the books of that event has the
somewhat suggestive item "for mending of the ropes iiij^d." leaving
ignorant people to suppose that the ringers in their joy had not
too softly pulled the ropes). At St. Dunstan's in the West (in
which parish Temple Bar stands), the ringers not only rang merry
peals, but they and their "bread and drynke" cost the large sum
of five shillings ; at St. Michael's, Cornhill, "iiij torches and iiij
lynckes on the Queenes nighte" cost five shillings and four pence;
but at St. Lawrence, Pountney, they rejoiced in another way, for
four preachers received twenty shillings. Outside London, in the
provinces the records also speak of the enthusiasm. The thanksgiving day at Chester was celebrated on the 19th, by a sermon at
the Cathedral, "all shoppes, tavernes and typlynge houses being
shutte up all that day leste through anye worldlye occasyion those
who were not fully grounded in good heale myght withdrawe themselves from that most godly actyon," and at Shrewsbury "all
people that daye kept it holy unto the Lord that had given her
majestye sutche Victorie."

The Queen's procession to St. Paul's is shewn as a head-piece
to the Stationers' Almanack for 1760. Another joyful celebration
was the Lord Mayor's pageant (Sir Martyn Calthrop being Mayor),
October 29th. The printed copy was registered at Stationers'
Hall, but not one is now known to be in existence. The banners
taken from the Armada, and sent by the Lord Admiral to Walsingham on the 25th August, were displayed at Paul's Cross on the 8th
of September following, and the next day on London Bridge—the
very same day that the Mayor and seven Aldermen of Bristol
signed and sent off to Lord Burghley a letter informing him he
had been elected High Steward of that City in the room of the
late Earl of Leicester.*

* Lansdowne MS. 56 (202). Leicester did not long survive his Tilbury

The animosities against the Spaniards did not cease with the death of Philip the Second in 1598. The Ambassador in London had a hard time of it, and every opportunity was taken to insult or injure him. In 1618 and 1621 Gondomar, the then representative, was the cause of serious riots. In the former year the Ambassador having ridden over a little boy, the mob proceeded to his house in Barbican,* and would soon have wrecked it, had not the Lord Mayor and Chief Justice Mountague arrived upon the scene. The curious part of the matter is, King James I. compelled the Lord Mayor to beg Gondomar's pardon, while seven boys were sentenced to pay £500 each, and suffer six months' imprisonment; but they were subsequently pardoned.

Having in as concise a form as possible, summarised the documentary evidence upon the rise and fall of the Spanish Armada, I shall now say a few words about the very interesting and valuable List of Names reprinted from the scarce quarto tract of 1798, issued by "Leigh and Sotheby, York Street, Covent Garden," a copy of which, having the Rev. Samuel Lyson's notes, is in my Collection. The original MS. cannot be found; the author or editor of it is unknown, but Mr. John Bruce of the State Paper Office, who in May 1798 compiled for the private use of the Privy Council a " Report on the arrangements which were made for the internal defence of these kingdoms when Spain by its Armada proposed the Invasion and Conquest of England," (a copy of which most valuable report, with special dedication, notes, and signed by Bruce, is also in my Collection), tells us that "from the names and orthography, the MS., which I have not seen, is probably authentic." I shall presently prove it is so without doubt.

exertions ; he died Sept. 4th. His "last letter" to the Queen is in S. P. Dom. 215 (65).

* I have in my MS. Collection the original Mortgage from Lord Willoughby d'Eresby to Sir Charles Mountague of this very house, then called "Willughbie House als the Barbican als Basecourte," in which is recited the lease to the Spanish Ambassador, for seven years, from 11th October, 1612, at a rent of £180 per annum, showing it to have been a good sized mansion.

Here, I cannot refrain from quoting Mr. Bruce's remarks upon
the loss of the MS. He says: " It is one among many similar
proofs of the losses to which the King's Archives have been
exposed from the want of the strict regulations under which they
ought to have been originally placed." All those persons, like
myself, who have daily to search among the records and
registers will quite agree with Mr. Bruce, and I for one have
cause continually to lament the careless manner in which the
musty old deeds and priceless documents, so valuable to our
history generally, and so indispensable to genealogical enquiry,
have been guarded by their proper custodians. From the Muni-
ment room of the family mansion, or the "rubbish" shed of
some public institution to the waste-paper shop, or the butter-
man's store, seems to have been but a step.* Some of my own
Collections (Pedigrees, Court Rolls, and official documents of all
kinds, and of inestimable value) have been rescued by me from
such sources, so I can speak with feeling in the cause. Speci-
mens of some I have already published for the benefit of man-
kind at large, and I yet hope to do a further service in this
direction; but one of the documents I have I cannot refrain
from mentioning in this place—it is the original Will of the first
and last Earl of Cleveland, never proved, but which explains one
of the most important mysteries in the Wentworth Pedigree, as
I was assured years ago by the late Col. Chester, LL.D., who
some time previously had compiled a Wentworth genealogy. I
may also mention that I have an official document proving that
Lord Macaulay, although he was given permission by the Corporation in 1855, to inspect the records of the City of London, never
did so. Why, is to me a mystery, seeing that the treasures at

* I would specially refer to the Cottonian and Harley MSS. in the British
Museum, the Magna Charta, &c. It may not be generally known that the
valuable collection of "Cæsar Papers" were rescued by Patterson the
Auctioneer from a butter shop, and were subsequently sold by him in 187
lots, at the St. Paul's Coffee house, St. Paul's Churchyard, December, 1757,
for £356 0s. 6d.—the majority of the volumes being sold at a few shillings
each !

Guildhall would have caused him to have wonderfully altered some of his opinions too carelessly expressed in his otherwise valuable History.

Notwithstanding the extraordinary conduct of Queen Elizabeth in her management of affairs during the eventful period of the Armada Invasion, and how miserly she controlled necessary expenditure, the debts of the country had increased to an alarming extent. From the 22nd December, 1587, to the 15th September, 1588, the estimated wages of the navy amounted to £45,857; and from Michaelmas 1587 to Lady-day 1588 the preparation and victualling of the ships amounted to £96,770, so that the total cost may be estimated at nearly £150,000, quite irrespective of furniture and fittings, as also of those vessels supplied by the different places in England. On the 9th August, 1588, there were under the control of the Lord Admiral and Lord Seymour, 119 sail, and 11,120 men.

To meet these and other charges, it was necessary to raise money quite independent of the subsidies or taxes, for it must be presumed, seeing the overwhelming evidence existing among the State Papers, that Imperial Taxation, then as now, was no easy burthen to the English ratepayer. Besides this there was the expense of the Army. While Admiral Howard was bitterly lamenting that the Queen had done her best to starve the seamen, and Hawkins wrote that there were actually due to the seamen for wages £19,000 in arrears, the Lords of the Council had written to the various Lieutenants of the Counties, saying there was a report that the men of the army had been unpaid for some time, the officers receiving the wages from the day of camping to the dissolution. Burleigh too was terribly hampered, for, until he could obtain permission from the Queen, he was quite unable to send even the £8,000 immediately required, notwithstanding that he bore the title of England's Lord Treasurer.

Large subsidies had already been granted. In May, 1588, there was due, upon an assessment of £108,350, some £36,000. Sir Christopher Hatton had acquainted Parliament, on the 22nd February, of the need of help, and it was then that a committee

was appointed to raise the money.   Among Lord Burghley's papers*
is a draught of " ye preamble for ye subsidy," a twelvemonth later,
and this document is interesting, because it bears the Lord
Treasurer's autograph corrections.   In it we are told : "Wee do further
consider how for ye accomplishing of these y^r honorable and princely
actions, ye greate and infinite charges yor Mat^ie hath sustained,
and yt especially ye last yeare, in preparing and maintening
so long time so puisant an army by sea, besides ye forces
assembled by land, for y^c wt^hstanding of ye two great and mighty
armies prepared, ye one in ye Low Countries ready to pass ye seas
unto this realme under ye Duke of Parma, and ye other brought
forth out of Spain under ye Duke of Medina wt^h intent by their
mighty joint forces, far exceeding all others in any memory of man
to have made a *full* bloody conquest of this realme, had not y^e
same been prevented through ye singular, yea miraculous goodness
of Almighty God and y^r Highness's said great preparations and
forces."

To make an extraordinary subsidy, and so ruin the nation at
one stroke, to meet the cost of the defence made against the Invasion, was too much even for Queen Elizabeth, so she adopted
a wiser and less repulsive course, she borrowed, by way of loan, of
the 2,416 of her subjects, as set forth in the printed list, out of the
36 counties in England, a sum approaching £75,000 ; an amount,
at that date, very considerable, and especially so after the extraordinary charges each county had already borne in making other
provision.   Now, it will be noticed that the list does not mention
the year this money was paid, although the dates of payment ranged
from the 4th February to the following December ; but I will show
the date to be 1589, and that the amount was raised to meet the
arrears, then due for the charges of the year previous.   The too
brief "introduction" to the printed list of 1798, simply tells us
that letters were sent by the Queen to Sir Francis Walsingham,
keeper of the Privy Seal, and by him directed to the Lieutenants
of the various counties, requiring the raising of the loan.   This was

* Lansd. MS., 58 (182).

the truth, for a copy of one of these Privy Seals I now print, and it will not only show the proceedings adopted, but prove, in every way, that the list is genuine.*

" By the Queene,

" Trusty and welbeloved, we greete you well. Wheras for the better wᵗʰ standing of the intended invasion of this realme, upon the greate preparacōns made by the King of Spayne, bothe by sea and land, the last yeare, the same having been such as the lyke was never prepared at any tyme against this Realme, we were enforced for the defence of the same and of our good and loving subjects to be at infinite charges, both by sea and land, especially for that the said intended invasion tended directly to the conquest of this realme, and finding also by such intelligence as we dayly receave that the lyke intent the next yeare by the said Kinget for the wthstanding wherof yt shalbe necessary for us to prepare both by sea and land, wᶜʰ cannot be pformed wᵗʰout greate charges. We have therfore thought yᵗ expedient, having alwaies found our good and loving subiects most ready upon such lyke occasions to furnish us by way of *loane* of some convenient porcōns of mony agreable wᵗʰ their estates (wᶜʰ we have and mynd alwaies to repay) to have recourse unto them in lyke maner at this present, and therfore, having made choyce in the severall ptes of our Realme of a number able to do us this kinde of service, wᶜʰ is not refused betwixt neighbor and neighbor Amongst this nomber we have pᵗiculerly named you, *Thomas Lawley*, for your ability and good will you bear to us and our Realme, to be one. Wherfore, we require you to pay to our use the sume of Twenty-fyve Pounds to such ꝑson, as by our Licuteunt of that county shal be named to you by his hand wryting. And these our Lr̄es of

* See also the Sussex Arch. Collections, Vol. i., p. 32—37 (for an annotated copy of the Sussex list), and Owen and Blakeway's History of Shrewsbury, Vol. i., p. 389.

† This projected second invasion is explained hereafter.

Pryvy Seale subscribed by the pty so named by our Lieutennt that shall receave the same, confessing the tyme of the Receipt thereof shalbe sufficient to bynd us our heirès and successors, duely to repay the said some to you or to yor assignes at thend of one yeare from the tyme of yor payment. Yeven under my Pryvy Seale at our Pallace of Westm^r, the xxth day of ffebruary, in the xxxjth yeare of our Reigne.

THO. KER.

To o^r trustie and welbeloved,
    Thomas Lawley, of the Cop-
    pies, gent."

Now a reference to the list of contributions from Shropshire, will show that Thomas Lawley paid the £25 on the 19th April, and upon the document is a receipt signed by " E. Leighton," so dated, and a further note endorsed : " Salopp, Quinto Maii, 1590. Repayed unto his assignes by Killigrew."

Another proof of the authenticity of the list will be found among Lord Burghley's papers in the British Museum.* It is endorsed : "a note of all the Prvie seales sentdowne in the begynnynge of Mche, 1588."—Lincolnshire. In this document there are 129 names ; in the printed list only 115, the fourteen excluded having a memorandum against them, such as "insufficient," "discharged," or (as in the case of " George Berry, of Carlesby ") " discharged by lrēs frō my Lō Tresor." The 115 names, with the amounts against each agree with the printed list, except in some instances as to spelling, which must be considered excusable at that date, seeing how often in important documents, such as wills, the name of the testator, will be found written in several ways.

The third proof is an original memorial to Secretary Wolly, in April, 1589, from one Matthew Chubb, of Dorchester, who will be found in the list of the county of Dorset, as being charged with £50 the 29th March. He prays an excuse for paying by reason that " neither the Lord Leutenant nor the Deputie Leutenants

---

* Lansdowne MS. 81 (141).

have certified the sufficiencie of yor suppliant to be able to *lend* her matie anie some of money."* This shews that it was a practice to charge individuals of supposed means without asking, and chance whether they paid or not.

During the months of May, June, and July, the Privy Council were continually sending letters to the collectors, requesting all arrears to be paid up. In Surrey £500 out of £2,000 remained unpaid, and, in one instance, on July 16th, 1589, it was argued that the great losses of sheep, cattle, and corn, had impoverished the would-be contributors.† From thirty counties, at the date ending June, £46,925 had been received. Among those who were proposed to be charged, were, gentlemen of the court, law, and crown; and lists of these are still preserved. Among those belonging to the King's Bench were seven officers and forty "fillizers and attornies," and in the list signed by Sir Christopher Wray, the Chief Justice, I find the first attorney named, to be none other than Miles Doddinge, so well known from the grants he had of "concealed lands." In another document we are told : "Sir James Harrington, Knight, collector for countie of Rutland, both paid only £275 of the £500 imposed upon that countie, whereof £100 assessed upon himself is also unpaide, being βcall of the £500," and a reference to the list will show that Rutland is assessed at £375. Gloucester was originally assessed at £4,000, but paid £2,475 "in respect of the povertie in the countrey by the murreyn of cattell, the rot of sheepe, and lacke of rent for cloth and corne." Buckingham was assessed at £3,000, but paid only £1,427. Somerset assessed at the like sum, paid £2,300, "for that many trayned souldiers and others being charged the last yeare were charged with this loane." In Lincoln : "Sir Anthony Thorold hath also signified that divers persons refuse to paye." Norfolk assessed at £5,000, only remitted to the collector £3,380. In fact, in a great number of cases the cry from those assessed was the answer flatly refusing, as "the lieutenants have not any commission to

---

* S. P. Dom. 223 (114).

† Molyneux Papers, Hist. MS., vii. (647).

warrant them doing in this behalfe." In one case the individual
assessed prayed that two persons should be joined for the payment
of the £25 named.

It will be seen, by these proofs that the list, reprinted from
the scarce 4to copy of 1798, is genuine, notwithstanding that the
original, from which it was transcribed, cannot now be found. It is
probably owing to this fact that those unused to the searching of
records have, hitherto, given the useful printed copy a bad name,
which I have now done my best to prove groundless. One of the
reasons given for doubting it, was that the City of London is not
mentioned in it, but this I explain : that the city contribution
formed quite a distinct loan ; it subscribed amongst the citizens belonging to the livery companies, no less than £54,000, or more
than two-thirds of the whole amount all England is shewn to have
paid, and a Bond given by Queen Elizabeth to the Corporation for
£30,000 is still extant. If another edition of this work is called
for, I shall be inclined to include in it the city list, and add such
other facts that want of space alone now prevents me printing.

I must now mention that Queen Elizabeth, being determined to
retaliate upon the Spaniards, and not wait for another Invasion
from them, but really, to invade the territory of King Philip instead, issued her commission to Sir John Norris and Sir Francis
Drake, early in 1589, and in the instructions were included the
appointment of Sir Roger Williams and Thomas Fenner, in the
room of Norris or Drake, if either should die. And by her letter,
dated Somerset House, 21 November, 1590, she asked for another
loan. This list is extant; it is equally extensive, and valuable,
and may be included in my next edition (together with much interesting information relating to it, preserved among the city archives), as a centenary volume some years hence.

In conclusion, I have only to add that the documents quoted
from have been examined, and this has proved no ordinary
labour, and but for valuable assistance rendered by my brother,
Mr. W. F. Noble, of Forest Hill Road, London, S.E., the work
could not have been accomplished so satisfactorily as it is—the
principal object in view being at the present time not only to write

an Historical Essay upon the rise and fall of the Armada, but also to prove that the printed list is genuine, and consequently of the greatest value to genealogists and county historians, while the Index will be found not only useful, but certainly an indispensable feature in the present publication.

T. C. NOBLE.

110, GREENWOOD ROAD,
    DALSTON, LONDON, E.,
        January, 1st, 1886.

The Names of Those who contributed to the Defence of this Country at the Time of the Spanish Invasion in 1588.

BEDFORDSHIRE.

		£.
March.	Walter Luke, Gen. 21 *die Marcii*... ...	25
	John Burgoyne, Armiger 25 *Marcii* ...	40
	Richard Charnock, Armiger 26 *Marcii* ...	40
	William Duncombe, Armiger *eodem* ...	40
	Phillip Johns, Gen. *eodem*	40
	John Clerke 31 *die Marcii*	25
	Richard Harding, Armiger *eodem*... ...	25
April.	Henrie Fairie *primo die Aprilis*	25
	Thomas Cheyney, Gen. 7 *Aprilis*... ...	40
	William Adams, Gen. *eodem*	25
	Thomas Hawes, Senior, Tanner *eodem* ...	25
	William Audeley 9 *die Aprilis*	25
	Thomas Parratt, Gen. 10 *Aprilis*... ...	25
	Thomas Ympie 11 *Aprilis*	25
	Christofer Estwicke 12 *Aprilis*	25
	Henry Lodge 14 *Aprilis*	25
	Robert Grigg, Yeoman 14 *Aprilis* ...	25
	Richard Crawley, Yeoman 15 *Aprilis* ...	25
	Nicholas Denton *eodem*	25
	William Stone, Armiger 16 *die Aprilis* ...	50
	Thomas Spicer, alias Alder 18 *die Aprilis* ...	25
	George Keaynsham, Armiger *eodem* ...	50
	Fraancis Farrer, Gen. *eodem*	25
	Humfrey Fitzwilliam, Armiger 24 *Aprilis* ...	25
Maye.	John Catesbie, Armiger *quinto die Maii* ...	25

B

£.

Maye.	Henrie Edwardes, Gen. 19 *Maii* ...	...	25
	John Crawley 22 *die Maii*	...	25
	William Clerke, Gen. 26 *die Maii*	...	25
	John Davie, Gen. 29 *die Maii*	...	25
June.	Oliver Skroggs, Gen. 9 *die Junii* ...	...	25
July.	Matthew Hanscombe 24 *die Julii* ...	...	25
	George Butler *the* 31 *of July*	...	25
	George Smyth *the same Daye*	...	25
August.	Roberte Bellamy th'elder *the* 3 *of August* ...		25

BERKSHIRE.

£.

Feb.	Edward Martyn *quarto die Februarii*	...	25
	Thomas Reade, Armiger *eodem* ...	...	50
	Humfrey Foster, Armiger *eodem* ...	...	50
	Oliver Ashcombe 16 *die Februarii*	...	25
	John Payne 18 *die Februarii*	...	25
	Edward Bacon *eodem* ...	...	25
	Thomas Goodman *eodem*	...	25
	William Dunche 25 *Februarii*	...	100
	John Organ 26 *die Februarii*	...	25
	James Stone *eodem*	...	25
	Christofer Marshall 27 *Februarii* ...	...	25
	John Planner *eodem*	...	25
	Clement Dawbney *eodem*	...	50
	William Dinton *eodem* ...	...	25
	Edmunde Wiseman 28 *of February*	...	25
	John Saunders *eodem* ...	...	25
March.	Nicholas Radishe *tercio die Marcii*	...	25
	Thomas Bellamye *eodem*	...	50
	William Nelson *quarto die Marcii*	...	25
	Richard Chock, *quinto die Marcii* ...	...	50
	Adam Blandie *sexto die Marcii* ...	...	25

		£.
March.	Roger Garrade *eodem*	25
	Thomas Pleydall *eodem*...	25
	William Blagrove *eodem*	25
	William Hide *eodem*	25
	John Smithe *eodem*	25
	Richarde Pocock 9 *Marcii*	25
	William Blackenholl 12 *Marcii*	25
	John Clarke 14 *die Marcii*	25
	Richard Davers 22 *Marcii*	25
	Thomas Mariott 24 *Marcii*	25
	Ladie Jane Duckett 26 *Marcii*	50
	Thomas Clerke *eodem*	25
	John Elston 27 *die Marcii*	25
April.	Anthonie Blagrove *quinto die Aprilis* ...	25
	Thomas Seymour *sexto die Aprilis* ...	25
	Richard Plott *eodem*	25
	Frauncis Winchecombe *eodem*	25
	John Pleydall 7 *Aprilis*...	25
	Frauncis Parkins *eodem*...	50
	William Hobbes 8 *Aprilis*	25
	Edmunde Fetiplace *eodem*	50
	Christofer Fetiplace *eodem*	25
	John Southbie 12 *Aprilis*	50
	Thomas Donington 14 *Aprilis*	25
	William Willmott *eodem*	25
	Thomas Chamberlyn *eodem*	25
	Henrie Newburie 15 *Aprilis*	25
	Robert Hutchins 18 *Aprilis*	25
Maye.	Edward Archer 23 *Maii*	25
	Walter Prane *eodem*	25
	Richard Hide *the* 26 *Maii*	25
	Richard Humfrey *eodem*	25
June.	John Doe 24 *Junii*	25
	James Grove *eodem*	25
	Frauncis Welskorne 26 *Junii*	25
July.	Richard Surie 24 *Julii*	25

			£.
July.	Henrie Slade *eodem*	25
	John Latton 26 *Julii*	25
August.	Roberte Hammonde 2 *of August*	25
	John Noyce 6 *of Augus:*	25
	Thomas Lyford 7 *of August*	25
Septemb.	John Lancaster 5 *of September*	25
	John Pledall 27 *of September*	25
October.	Michaell Penyston *primo die October* ...	25
	John Keale 24 *of October*	25
	Pawle Ortewoode 25 *of October*	25
	John Staunton 28 *of October*	25
	Henry Smith *eodem*	25
	John Buckeridge 29 *of October*	25
	John Whichlowe *eodem*...	25
	Roger Higgs *eodem*	25
	Richard Allen *eodem*	25
	Nicholas Badcocke *eodem*	25
	John Sherewood *eodem*	25
	Andrew Stevenson *eodem*	25
	John Jennyngs *eodem*	25
	Richard Webbe 30 *of October*	25
	Gabriell Cocks 31 *of October*	25

BUCKINGHAMSHIRE.

		£.
Feb.	Frauncis Lovett, Gen. 20 *die Februarii* ...	25
	John Rotheram, Armiger 27 *die Februarii* ...	25
	Dame Dorothie Pelham, Vidua *ultimo Februarii*	50
March.	Walter Courson, Gen. *primo die Marcii* ...	25
	John Fountaine, Gen. *sexto die Marcii* ...	25
	William Winloe, Gen. 14 *die Marcii* ...	25
	John Dormer, Gen. 15 *die Marcii* ...	25

                                            £.

		£.
March.	Frauncis Howse, Gen. 17 *die Marcii* ...	25
	Thomas Duncombe, of Great Brickell 18 *die Marcii*	25
	Edmonde Duncombe, Gen. 21 *die Marcii* ...	23
	John Deverell *eodem*	25
	John Duncombe, of Barliende, Gen. *eodem* ...	25
	Edmonde West, of Marsworth, Gen. *eodem* ...	50
	William Cockman, of Ailisburie 23 *Marcii* ...	25
	Thomas Bowlinge, Sen. *eodem*	25
	Richard Howse 24 *die Marcii*	25
	Frauncis Pigott, Gen. *eo em*	25
	John Doncombe, of Wingrave, Sen. 26 *Marcii*	25
	William Brittridge, of Iver, Gen. 28 *Marcii*	50
	William Hobbes, of Westwicombe, *ultio die Marcii*	25
Aprill.	Dorothie Gamage, Vidua *primo die Aprilis*...	25
	John Cheyney, Gen. *eodem*	25
	Thomas Potts, Gen. *quinto die Aprilis* ...	25
	Richard Chitwood, Armiger *eodem* ...	25
	Richard Ingolsbie, Gen. 8 *die Aprilis* ...	25
	John Doncombe, of Dinton, Gen. 9 *Aprilis*...	25
	Thomas Jakeman, of Winge 12 *Aprilis* ...	25
	Richard Saunders, Gen. 14 *Aprilis* ...	25
	Benedicte Winchcombe, Gen. 17 *Aprilis* .	25
	Thomas Duncombe, of East Claidon, Gen. 23 *Aprilis*	25
	Thomas Saunders, of Dinton, Gen. 24 *Aprilis*	25
	George Moore, Gen. 29 *die Aprilis* ...	25
Maye.	William Moulsoe, Gen. *primo die Maii* ...	25
	Richard Trowghton, Gen. *secundo die Maii*...	25
	Edmonde Foster. Gen. *eodem*	25
	William Mountgomery, Gen. *tercio die Maii*...	25
	Rowlande Hinde, Gen. *eodem*	25
	Richard Chubnoll, Gen. *quarto die Maii* ...	27
	Thomas Barenger. *septimo die Maii* ...	25
	George Woodward, Gen. 9 *die Maii* ...	25
	Richard Weedon *decimo die Maii*... ...	25
	John Wade, of Culverton 17 *Maii* ...	25
	Thomas Aishfeild, Armiger 19 *Maii* ...	50
	James Stevens *eodem*	25

				£.
Maye.	John Lambert 20 *die Maii*			25
	Leonard Pigott 21 *die Mari*			25
June.	John Briscoll *the* 10 *day of June*			25
	George Curter 26 *of June*			25
July.	John Coffenden, alias Slater *the seconde day of July*			25
	Richard Bloode *the* 30 *of July*			25
August.	Henry Longevile 3 *of August*			25
	Roberte Mordant *the* 31 *of August* ...			50

CANTABRIGIA

		£.
Feb.	Edward Barnes, Gen. 24 *Februarii* ...	25
	John Cropley *eodem*	25
	Henrie Seaman *eodem*	25
	John Grayve, Sen. of Fordham *eodem* ...	25
	John Pratt, of Wooditton *eodem*	25
	John Folkes, of Swafham Bulbeck *eodem* ...	25
	Edmund Bacchus, of Swafham Prior *eodem*...	25
	Thomas Smithe, of Stowe *eodem*	25
	Edward Styward, Armiger, of Feversham *eodem*	50
	George Foster. Gen. of Bottesham 24 *Februarii*	25
	Edward Wood, Gen. of Fulborne *eodem* ...	25
	Thomas Hancock, Sen. of Fulborne, *eodem* ...	25
	Richard Hasill, of Balshaw *eodem* ...	25
	Gilbert Wise, of Hinton *eodem*	25
	Thomas Burie, of Horsheath *eodem* ...	25
	Richard Davie, of Sawston *eodem*... ...	25
	Edward Howsden, of Hinxton *eodem* ...	25
	Robert Swann, of Icleton...	25
	William Tharbie, Sen. of Witlesford *eodem*...	25
	Thomas Hodilowe, of Cambridg *eodem* ...	25
	John Batisford, Gen. of Chesterton *eodem* ...	50
	William Carrowe, of Chesterton *eodem* ...	25
	John Martin, Gen. of Barton *eodem die* ...	100

£.

Feb.

John Chaplyn, of Trumpington *eodem* ...	25
Katheryn Whale, Vidua, of Thriplowe *eodem*	25
John Taylor, of Thriplowe *eodem*... ...	25
Edward Aldred, of Fulmeare *eodem* ...	25
Walter Pilgryme, of Windie *eodem* ...	25
Thomas Cropwell, of Bourne *eodem* ...	25
Seth Warde, of Abington juxta Shingey *eodem*	25
Thomas Lilley, of Gilden Morden *eodem* ...	25
Nicholas Johnson, alias Butler, of Orwell *eodem*	25

Aprill.

Robert Pratt, of Melreath 15 *Aprilis* ...	25
Walter Hitch, of Melbourne *eodem* ...	25
Barbara Snell, Vidua, of Royston *eodem* ...	25
Thomas Peck, of Eversden *eodem*... ...	25
John Marshall, of Eltisley *eodem*... ...	25
Adam Thurgood, of Eltisley	25
John Bolnest, of Litlington *eodem* ...	25
Thomas Holliwell, of Weavlingham *eodem* ...	25
Henric Graype, of Weavlingham *eodem* ...	25
William Gery, Gen. of Over *eodem die* ...	25
William Iley, of Over *eodem*	25
William Steven, of Over *eodem*	25
Johan Maldric, Vidua, of Papworth Agnis *eodem*	25
William Peck, of Hardwick *eodem die* ...	25
John Stewkyn, of Longstanton *eodem die* ...	25

Maye.

Richard Richardes, of Mylton 29 *die Maii* ...	25
William Agnes, of Landbeach *eodem* ..	25
Robert Peach, of Fendrayton *eodem* ...	25
John Barton, of Fendraiton *eodem* ...	25
William March, Gen. of Ely *eodem* ...	25
Daniell Goodrick, Gen. of Ely *eodem* ...	25
John Martyn, of Elye *eodem*	25
John Daie, Jun. of Elie *eodem*	25
William Crauford, of Elie *eodem*... ...	25
Edward Marche, of Elye *eodem*	25
Thomas Wade, of Litelport *eodem* ...	25
John Kirkes, of Hadenham *eodem* ...	25
John Bernard, of Hadenham *eodem* ...	25

£.

Maye.	John Thurgood, Sen. of Wicham *eodem* ...	25
	Edward Homerston, of Coveney *eodem* ...	25
	John Reade, Sen. of Chatteris *eodem* ...	25
	William Sturmyn, of Wisbitch 29 *Maii* ...	25
	William Skootred, of Wisbitch *eodem* ...	25
	Thomas Phage, of Marche 29 *Maii* ...	25
	Robert Girdeou, of Wisbitch *eodem* ...	25
Junii.	Edmunde Laverocke, of Upwell 20 *die Junii*	25
	James Sallibaucke, of Wisbitche *eodem* ...	25
	Robert Lyne, of Wisbitch *eodem* ...	25
	Robert Cowper, of Wisbitch *eodem* ...	25
	Arthur Dalton, of Wisbitch *eodem* ...	25
	Thomas Jones, of Leverington ...	25
	Symon Treane, of Newton *eodem* ...	25
	John Bonde, of Persondrove *eodem* ...	25

CHESHIRE.

£.

Feb.	Peter Warburton, Armiger 18 *Februarii* ...	21
	Thomas Leigh, of High Leigh, Armiger 24 *Februarij*	50
	John Leigh, of Boothe, Armiger 31 *Februarij* (?)	25
	Thomas Tutchett. Armiger 24 *Februarij* ...	25
	Thomas Leigh, of Adlington, Arm. 21 *Februarij*	25
	Henrie Berkenhead, Armiger 14 *Februarii* ...	25
	Richard Grávnor, Armiger 25 *Februarii* ..	25
	Sir William Brereton, Miles *eodem* ...	100
	Phillip Oldefield 27 *Februarii* ...	25
	The Ladie Egerton 20 *Februarii* ...	50
	Thomas Wilbram, Armiger 15 *die Februarii*	25
March.	George Booth, Armiger 11 *Marcii* ...	25
	Randall Manwering, of Peever, Armiger 9 *Marcii*	25
	John Dutton, Armiger *secundo die Mercii* ...	25
	Thomas Aston, Armiger *quarto die Marcii* ...	25
	William Marbury, of Meare, Armiger *primo die Marcij*	25
	Adam Leicester, Armiger 11 *Marcii* ...	25
	Sii Peter Leigh, Miles 16 *Marcii* ...	100

£.

March. William Brereton, of Handford, Armiger   16 *Marcii* 25
William Davenport, of Bromhall, Armiger 19 *Marcii* 25
Thomas Standley, of Alderley, Armiger   *quarto die*
Marcii   25
Randall Davenport, of Henbry, Armiger 14 *Marcii* 25
William Duckensfield, Armiger 17 *Marcii* ...   25
Raphe Harden, Armiger   *eodem*   25
Rodert Hid, of Norbry, Armiger 13 *Marcii*   25
Sir Randall Brereton, Miles 6 *Marcii* ...   50
Hugh Calverley, of Ley, Armiger 27 *Marcii*   50
Rowland Dutton, Armiger 17 *Marcii* ...   25
Ralph Calveley, Armiger 11 *Marcii* ...   25
The Ladie Boothe *tercio die Marcii* ...   25
The Ladie Warburton *eodem*   25
Henrie Manwering, Armiger *quarto die Marcii*   25
Geffrey Shakerley, Armiger 9 *die Marcii* ...   25
Sir Rowland Standeley, Miles 7 *Marcii* ...   100
George Massey *sexto die Marcii*   25
John Poole, Armiger 9 *die Marcii* ...   25
Thomas Bunburie, Armiger *primo die Marcii*   25
William Whitmore, Armiger *tercio die Marcii*   25
John Egerton, Armiger 22 *Marcii* ...   `25
John Browne, of Stapleford *quarto die Marcii*   25
Henrie Delves, Armiger 24 *Marcii* ...   25
Richard Cotton, Armiger 17 *Marcii* ...   25
Thomas Vernon, Armiger 13 *Marcii* ...   25
Jo. Griffith, Armiger 25 *Marcii*   25
Roger Manwering 17 *Marcii*   25
Richard Wilbram *eodem die*   25
Richard Church *eodem*   25
Geffrie Minshull *eodem*   25

Aprill. Thomas Brooke, Armiger 9 *die Aprilis* ...   25
Thomas Venables, Armiger 11 *die Aprilis* ...   25

Maye. Tho. Smithe, Armiger 25 *die Maii* ...   25

C

CORNWALL.

			£.
March.	John Kympthorne, Armiger 26 *of Marche* ...		25
	John Buggens *eodem*		25
	Sampson Srilles *eodem*		25
	Oliver Sawle *eodem*		25
	Thomas Hext, of Launston 27 *Marcii* ...		25
	John Roberts 28 *Marcii*		100
	Richard Roberts *eodem*		25
	William Marke 29 *Marcii*		25
Aprill.	Thomas Mayo, of Menhenet 8 *Aprilis* ...		25
	Walter Burlace, Gent. *eodem*		25
	Robert Trencreke, Armiger 11 *Aprilis* ...		50
	Robert Smithe, Gent. *eodem*		50
	Richard Chamonde, Armiger *eodem* ...		50
	John Brode *eodem die*		25
	John Mayo, alias Helier *eodem*		25
	George Kekewith, Armiger *eodem*		25
May.	Edward Skawen *sexto die Maii*		25
	Frauncis Buller, Arm. *eodem*		50
	Philip Maie *eodem*		25
	John Coade, Gen. *eodem*		25
	William Bodie *eodem*		25
	Thomas Clief *eodem*		50
	William Pascow *eodem*		25
June.	Edward Noye 21 *Junii*		25
	*George Roolles, Armiger *eodem*		25
	*John Arundell, of Swernacke, Armiger ...		50
	*John Prideaux, of Padstowe, Armiger ...		25

DERBY.

			£.
March.	John Harpur, Armiger 26 *die Marcij* ...		50
	John Bullock, Armiger *eodem*		50

* Not charged.

£.

March.		£.
	Thomas Gell, Armiger *eodem*	50
	John Fraunces, Armiger *eodem*	25
	Leonard Shallcrosse, Gen. *eodem*	25
	James Abney, Armiger *eodem*	25
	Constance Edmundson, Vidua *eodem* ...	25
	Thomas Leigh, of Egginton, Armiger *eodem*	25
	Walter Horton, of Catton, Armiger *eodem* ...	25
	William Blackwall, of Alton, Gen. *eodem* ...	25
	Michaell Willoughby, of Risley *eodem* ...	25
	William Colledg, of Steede, Gen.	25
	John Merry, of Barton, Gen.	25
	Humfrey Dethicke, of Newall, Armiger *eodem*	25
	Arthur Porter, of Howne, Gen. *eodem* ...	25
	Richard Dale of Osmaston *eodem*.. ...	25
	Sir Tho. Kokeyne, Knight 27 *Marcii* ...	50
	John Dethick, of Bredsall, Gen. *eodem* ...	25
	Thomas Knyveton, of Mercaston, Armiger *eodem*	25
	Mrs. Fretchvile, of Stanley, Vidua *eodem* ...	25
	Robert Sitwell, of Stanley, Gen. *eodem* ...	25
	Henrie Bagshawe, of Ridge, Gen. *eodem* ...	25
	Roberte Baynebridge, of Calke, Gen. *eodem*	25
Aprill.	Thomas Greasley, Armiger *quarto die Aprilis*	25
	Mrs. Fielding, of Derby, Vidua *eodem* ...	25
	Henrie Wigley, of Midleton, Gen. *eodem* ...	25
	Thomas Moseley, of Eyam *quinto die Aprilis*	25
	Thomas Eire, of Highlowe, Gen. *eodem* ...	25
	Richard Kirkeland, of Normanton *eodem* ...	25
	Henrie Kendall, of Smythesby, Gen. *eodem*...	25
	William Bassett, of Langley, Armiger *eodem*	25
	John Cley, of Wakebridge, Gen. *eodem* ...	25
	Godfrey Folliambe, of Walton, Armiger *eodem*	50
	John Longe, of Howne, Gen. *eodem* ...	25
	William Botham, of Derby, Draper *eodem* ...	25
	Richard Fletcher, of Derby, Butcher *eodem*	25
	George Revill, of Normanton, Gen. *eodem* ...	25
	Christofer Sclater, of Balbrough 8 *die Aprilis*	25
	John Gill, of Norton *eodem*	25
	John Parker, of Norton, Gen. 9 *die Aprilis*	25

		£.
Aprill.	John Rodes, of Staley, Armiger *eodem* ...	25
	Edwarde Smithe, of Derby, Butcher 12 *Aprilis*	25
	James Lynacre, Armiger 14 *Aprilis* ...	25
	Roger Columble, of Derbie, Gen. *eodem* ...	25
	Robert Spencer, of Glapwell 20 *Aprilis* ...	25
June.	Adam Beresford, Gen. 15 *Junii*	25
	Walter Powndrell, Armiger, and his Mother 18 *die Junii*	25
Julye.	Fraunces Leake *the* 8 *of Julye*	50

DEVON.

		£.
Aprill.	John Newcorte *quarta die Aprilis*... ...	25
	Richard Gilbert 8 *die Aprilis*	25
	Robert Avery *eodem*	25
	Thomas Wise, Armiger *eodem*	50
	John Parker, Armiger *eodem*	25
	William Harrys *eodem*	50
	Walter Heale *eodem*	50
	Edmond Raynell 9 *Aprilis*	25
	John Welshe *eodem*	25
	William Strowde *eodem die*	25
	Leonard Yeo *eodem*	25
	William Dennys, of Orleigh *eodem* ...	25
	Thomas Hunt, of Chudley *eodem*... ...	25
	William Abbot *eodem*	50
	Alexander Knapman *eodem*	25
	Nicholas Sperke, of Dunsford *eodem* ...	25
	Robert Davie *eodem*	25
	Hugh Heale *eodem*	25
	Henrie Copelston	50
	Thomas Bartlett *eodem*	25
	Thomas Elford *eodem*	25
	Thomos Melhinche *eodem*	25
	Roger Walker *eodem*	25

					£.
Aprill.	Humfrey Specott *eodem*...	...	...		50
	Nicholas Glanvile *eodem*	...	...		50
	Arthur Copleston *eodem*	...	...		25
	George Pyne *eodem*	...	...		25
	William Ashe *eodem*	...	...		50
	William Greenes *eodem* ...	...	...		50
	Nicholas Predeaux 10 *Aprilis*	...	...		25
	John Phillippes *eodem* .	...	...		25
	John Moore *eodem*	...	...		25
	Arthur Arscott *eodem* ...	...	...		25
	Lawrence Radforde *eodem*	...	...		50
	William Poole, Armiger *eodem*	...	...		25
	Thomas Southcott, Armiger *eodem*	...			50
	William Waldron, Armiger *eodem*...	...			50
	John Stuckley, Armiger *eodem*	...	...		25
	John Davie, of Crediton *eodem*	...	...		25
	Arthur Trobridge *eodem*	...	...		25
	Thomas Quicke *eodem* ...	...	...		25
	John Gifford *eodem*	...	...		25
	Roger Costurd *eodem* ...	...	...		25
	Phillip Courteney *eodem*	...	...		25
	John Davie 11 *Aprilis* ...	...	...		25
	George Carie, Armiger *eodem*	...	...		25
	Davie Moore *eodem* ...	...	...		25
	John Fitz, Armiger *eodem*	...	...		50
	Geffrey Babb *eodem* ...	...	...		50
	Eustace Stowell *eodem* ...	...	...		25
	William Hurst *eodem* ...	...	...		50
	William Peter, Armiger ...	...	...		25
	John Sweete *eodem* ...	...	...		25
	George Gale *eodem* ...	...	...		25
	Odes Peter *eodem* ...	...	...		50
	Lawrence Sheldon *eodem*	...	...		25
	William Hawkins *eodem die*	...	...		25
	Roger Beaple *eodem* ...	...	...		25
	Henrie Rowles 13 *Aprilis*	...	...		50
	John Bounde, of Iplepen *eodem* ...		...		25
	John Sweteland *eodem* ...	...	...		25
	Richard Steere 17 *die Aprilis*	...	...		25

		£.
April.	Walter Buggens *eodem* ...	50
	John Fortescue 18 *Aprilis*	25
	Nicholas Goodridge 19 *die Aprilis*	50
	Henrie Luscombe 20 *Aprilis*	25
	John Coffin, Arm. 22 *Aprilis*	25
	William Spealte 24 *Aprilis*	25
	John Putt 25 *die Aprilis*	25
	Geffrye Bulley *ultimo die Aprilis* ...	25
	John Wise *eodem*	25
	Christofer Savery *eodem*...	25
	Nicholas Hayman *eodem die*	25
Maye.	John Furse *secundo die Maii*	25
	Edward Golde *quinto die Maii*	25
	Thomas Caunter, of Stannerton *eodem*	25
	William Fortescue, of Wood *sexto die Maii*...	50
	Thomas Rudgwaie *eodem*	50
	Thomas Doclon 21 *die Maii*	25
	William Brawley 21 *die Maii*	25
	George Smithe *eodem*	50
	Henrie Ellacott *eodem*	25
	Walter Heale 30 *die Maii*	25
	Richard Brooking *eodem*	25
	Richard Bamfield, Armiger	25
	Peter Halstooke 30 *Maii*	25
	Henry Woode *eodem*	25
July.	Christopher Gover 11 *Julii*	25
	Thomas Brutt ...	25
	Prestwood	25
	Christofer Blackafler 19 *Julii*	25
	Richard Blackaller *eodem*	25
	John Steere 26 *Julii*	50
August.	John Skynner *the 6 of August*	25
	William Buckforde *the same daie* ...	25
	Edward Meredith *the same day*	25
	Thomas Stokes *the same daie*	25
	John Blundell *the 18 of August*	25

		£.
August.	Nicholas Spicer *the same day*	25
October.	Sherman *the first of October* ...	25
	John Copleston *the 10 of October*	25
	Thomas West *the 11 of October*	25
	Nicholas Cove *the 14 of October*	25
	William Catteforde *the 18 of October* ...	25
	Leonard Myller *the 28 of October*	25
	Giles Balle *the same day*	25
	John Stooke *the 23 of October*	25
	William Even *the same day*	25
	John Upton *the 6 of August*	25

DORSETT.

		£.
Feb.	Thomas Moreton, of Clenston 24 *die Februarij*	50
	Henrie Uvedall, of Moorccrichell, Armiger 25 *Februarii*	50
Marcii.	Henrie Brewen, of Athelhamston, Armiger *primo Marcii*	50
	John Studley, of Petersham, Gen. 8 *Marcii* ...	25
	William Webb, of Motcombe, Gen. 12 *Marcii*	50
	Roberte Freake, of Cearne Abbas, Armiger *eodem*	100
	Sir Matthew Arundell, Knight 13 *Marcii* ...	100
	John Miller, of Came, Gen. 14 *Marcii* ...	100
	Richard Pitt, of Melcomb Regis, Merchant *eodem*	25
	Henrie Coker, of Mapowder, Armiger 15 *Marcii*	100
	Ralphe Hardinge, of Longe Breddie, Gen. *eodem*	50
	William Churchell, of Dorchester, Merchant 17 *Marcii*	50
	Roberte More, of Wareham, Gen. 20 *die Marcii*	25
	Richard More, of Ockford cum Keyworth 22 *Marcii*	25
	Roberte Harbyn, of Stalbridge, Gen. *eodem* ...	100

		£.
March.	Thomas Chafyn, of Foke, Armiger 24 *Marcii*	100
	James Hannam, of Caundlepurse, Armiger *eodem*	100
	Edward Man, of Poole 24 *Marcii*... ...	25
	John Seymour, of Stoke Wake, Gen. 26 *Marcii*	25
	William Prowte, of Letton, Gen. 29 *Marcii*...	25
	Matthew Chubb, of Dorchester *eodem* ...	50
	Jane Serger, of Shurborne, Vidua *ultimo die Marcii*	25
Aprill.	John Jones, of Lyme Regis, Merchant *primo die Aprilis*...	50
	William Symondes, of Lyme Regis, Merchant *eodem*	25
	John Rawles, of Fifehead *eodem*	50
	Richard Chapman, of Lamton *eodem* ..	25
	Gyles Symondes, of Woodford, Gen. *secundo die Aprilis*...	25
	John Swayne, of Blandford, Gen. *tercio die Aprilis*	25
	John Skerne, of Turners Piddle, Gen. *eodem*...	25
	John Loope, of Hide *quarto die Aprilis* ...	25
	George Lambert, of Henburie *eodem* ...	50
	Thomazin Turbervile, of Beere Regis, Vidua *sexto Aprilis*	25
	Richard Sidwaie, of Poole 9 *Aprilis* ...	25
	Thomas Watts, of Stalbrige *eodem* ...	25
	John Williams, of Tyneham, Gen. 19 *Aprilis*	25
	Edward Hooper, of Beveridge 25 *Aprilis* ...	25
	Richard Eastmonde, of Fifehead Magdalen *eodem*	25
	Morgan Hayne, of Fryar Waddon 26 *Aprilis*	25
May.	Thomas Evans, of Muncton 13 *die Maii* ...	25
	Henry Stoite, of Milton 15 *die Maii* ...	25
	John Hoskins, of Bemister, Gen. 28 *die Maii*	25
June.	Christopher Darby, of Askerwell 7 *Junii* ...	25
	Thomas Savadge, of Sidling 9 *Junii* ...	25
	Phillip Mannfeild, of Shurborne 25 *Junii* ...	25

£.

Septemb. Hugh Whetcombe, of Shurbornc, 18 *die Septembris*   25

Novemb. William Gowld, of Gussage, Gen.   11 *Novembris*   25
         Thomas Scovell, of Wichampton   *eodem*   ...   25

DURHAM.

£.

Aprill. John Heath, *the* 12 *of Aprill* 25
William Lawson   *the same day* 25
Christofer Chater   *the same day* 25
John Clopton   *the same day* 25
Thomas Caverley   *the same day* 25
John Headworth   *the same day* 25
Raphe Taylboyes   *the same day* 25
Richard Bellaces   *the* 19 *of Aprill* 25
Raphe Lampton   *the same day* 25
Richard Conyers   *the same day* 25
William Blaxton   *the same day* 25
Nicholas Tempest   *the same day* 25
Richard Natres   *the same day* 25
Alexander Pingell   *the same pays* 25
Thomas Dacom   *the same daye* 25
George Frevyle   *the* 21 *day of Aprill* ... 25
Elizabeth Jennyson   *the same daye* ... 25
Thomas Salwyn   *the* 26 *of Aprill* 25

Maye. William Hodgson   *the third of May* ... 25
John Conyers   *the* 5 *of Maye* 25
William Blaxton   *the same day* 25
William Claxton   *the same day* 25
Dame Jane Bowes   *the same day* 25
Humfrey Blaxton   *the same daye* 25
Anthonye Welbury   *the same daye* ... 25
William Hall   *the same daye* 25
John Sampson   *the same daye* 25
Thomas Radclyffe   *the same daye* 25
Anthony Wren   *the* 11 *of Maye* 25
Henry Killinghall   *the* 12 *of Maye* 25
Barbary Blaxton   *the* 20 *of Maye* 25

D

£.

Maye.	Henry Lawson *the same daye*	25
	John Fetherstonhaughe *the* 31 *of Maye* ...	25
June.	Sir William Bowes *tne* 7 *of June*	25
	George Lightfoote *the* 23 *of June*	25

ESSEX.

£.

Feb.	The Ladie Frauncis Powlett, Vidua 6 *die Februarii*	50
	Raphe Wiseman, Armiger 7 *die Februarii*	100
	Abell Clarke, Gen. 11 *die Februarii* ...	25
	Richard Barlee, Armiger 12 *Februarii* ...	50
	John Driver *eodem*	25
	Henrie Collen 13 *die Februarii*	25
	Henrie Meriton 12 *die Februarii*	25
	William Adams 14 *die Februarii*	25
	Thomas Staples *eodem*	25
	George Wilmore 15 *Februarii*	25
	William Herd 16 *die Februarii*	25
	Richard Skevington, Gen. 17 *Februarii* ...	50
	Thomas Sutton, Armiger 18 *die Februarii* ...	100
	John Sammes, Gen. *eodem*	100
	William Vernon, Gen. *eodem*	25
	Thomas Myldmaie, Armiger *eodem* ...	50
	Thomas Bendishe, Armiger 22 *die Februarii*	100
	William Brocke, Gen. *eodem*	50
	John Greene 24 *die Februarii*	50
	John Skelton *eodem*	25
	John Wright, of the Bridge 25 *die Februarii*	50
	George Daie *eodem*	25
	Thomas Younge 26 *die Februarii* ...	25
	John Brett 27 *die Feburarii*	50
	Frauncis Ramme, Gen. 28 *Februarii* ...	25
	Thomas French *eodem*	25
	Thomas Rawlyn 7 *Februarii*	50
	Mathew Barnarde *eodem*	25
	Thomas Stokes *eodem*	25
	John Pic *eodem*	50

		£.
March.	John Wright, of Keldon *primo die Marcii* ...	50
	Robert Aylett *eodem*	25
	Thomas Emery *secundo die Marcii* ...	25
	John Skeale *tercio die Marcii*	25
	Nicholas Wall *eodem*	25
	Roberte Aylett, of Coggishall *eodem* ...	25
	Thomas Hopper *eodem*	25
	William Creswell *quinto die Marcii* ...	50
	Thomas Sayer *eodem*	25
	Roberte Noble 6 *die Marcii*	55
	Myles Bridget *eodem*	25
	John Bynkkes *eodem*	50
	Henrie Gaywood *eodem*...	25
	Richard Lambert 7 *die Marcii*	25
	Robert Mott *eodem dis*	25
	Thomas Barlowe *eodem*...	25
	Robert Potter *eodem*	25
	Henrie Reade *eodem*	25
	William Fuller *eodem*	25
	Roberte Winche 10 *Marcii*	25
	Thomas Sampford 11 *die Marcii*... ...	25
	Richard Evered *eodem*	50
	John Armonde 13 *die Marcii*	25
	John Liddiat *eodem*	25
	Edward Bullocke *eodem*	50
	William Tiffyn, Gen. *eodem*	25
	Arthur Breame, Gen. 14 *die Marcii* ...	50
	John Bedle *eodem*	25
	John Bacon *eodem*	25
	Isarell Amice, Armiger 15 *die Marcii* ...	50
	John Walker *eodem*	25
	William Sorrell *eodem*	25
	John Searle 19 *Marcii*	50
	George Noddes *eodem*	25
	Henrie Standishe *eodem*	25
	Roberte Brown 26 *Marcii*	25
	Thomas Lawrence *eodem*	25
	William Wiseman, of Brodokes, Armiger 27 *Marcii*	50
	Gabriell Pointz, Armiger *eodem*	50

		£.
Aprill.	Robert Kempe, Armiger 10 *die Aprilis* ...	50
	Thomas Wiberd *eodem*	25
	Roberte Agnes, alias Smithe 11 *die Aprilis*	25
	Christofer Somner 12 *die Aprilis*	25
	William Somner *eodem*	25
	Henrie Luckyn 15 *die Aprilis*	25
	Thomas Wilson, Gen. *eodem*	25
	Margery Edmondes, Vidua 17 *die Aprilis* ...	50
	Edward Chaplyn 19 *Aprilis*	25
	Henrie Bigge *eodem*	25
	James Richardson *eodem*	25
	Edmonde Churche, Gen. *eodem*	25
	Thomas Clarke *eodem*	25
	Robert Newman *eodem*	25
	Richard Raynsford. Gen. *eodem*	25
	The Ladie Judde, Vidua 19 *die Aprilis* ...	50
	John Friar, Gen. *eodem*	25
	Roberte Golding 15 *die Aprilis*	25
	Anthonie Roper, Armiger 20 *Aprilis* ...	25
	John Ive, Armiger *eodem*	50
	Thomas Turner 21 *die Aprilis*	25
	John Harrison 22 *die Aprilis*	25
	Katherin Audeley, Vidua *eodem*	50
	Richard Josua 24 *Aprilis*	25
	John Jackman, Armiger *eodem* ...	50
	Edward Glascock, Gen. 25 *Aprilis* ...	50
Maye.	Richard Jennyns, Gen. *primo die Maii* ...	25
	John Wiseman, of Stisted, Gen. *secundo die Maii*	25
	Richard Champion, Armiger *quarto die Maii*	50
	William Bright 7 *die Maii*	25
	Edward Elliot, Arm. 8 *die Maii*	25
	William Woodall, Gen. 9 *die Maii* ...	50
	Thomas Cropley *eodem*	25
	William Lande, Gen. *eodem*	25
	Mathew Alleston 14 *of Maie*	25
	Edward Riche 14 *Maii*	25
	John Lake 19 *die Maii*	25
	Henrie Glascock, Gen. *eodem*	25

		£
Maye.	Gyles Allen, Armiger 25 *Maii*	50
	John Roche, Gen. 26 *Maii*	100
	William Luckyn 29 *Maii*	50
June.	Leonard Aylett 7 *die Junii*	25
	Thomas Richmonde, Gen. 10 *Junii*	25
	William Strachey, Gen. 11 *Junii*	50
	Richard Osborne, Gen. 18 *Junii*	25
	Gyles Allen 25 *die Junii*	25
July.	John Everley *quarto die Julii*	25
	John Levitt *eodem*	25
	John Argent *eodem*	25

GLOUCESTER.

		£
March.	John Sidenham, of Frampton, Armiger *primo die Marcii*	25
	Paule 'Tracie, of Stanwaie, Arm. *quinto die Marcii*	50
	Alice Stratford, Vidua *eodem*	25
	William Hobby, of Hales, Armiger *eodem* ...	25
	John Trotman 11 *die Marcii*	25
	Richard Martyn *eodem die*	25
	John Woodwarde *eodem*	25
	Mathew Pointz, Armiger 12 *die Marcii* ...	25
	William Dutton, Armiger *eodem*	25
	John Bromage, of Bramsbarrow 15 *die Marcii*	25
	Edmonde Helmes, of Odington, Gen. 17 *die Marcii*	25
	Richard Bridges, of Combe 29 *Marcii*	25
Aprill.	Thomas Neale, of Yate *quinto die Aprilis* ...	25
	George Gough, of Hughelfield, Gen. 7 *Aprilis*...	25
	Walter Everarde, of Slimbridge 8 *die Aprilis* ...	25
	Thomas Estcourt, of Shipton, Armiger *eodem*...	25
	Thomas Bayneham, of Clowerwell *eodem* ...	25
	John Browne, of the Cittie of Glouc. Mercer ...	25
	Edward Michell, of the same, Gen. *eodem die*	25
	John Brewster, alias Skynner, of the same ...	25

		£
Aprill.	Richard Hardinge, of Slymbridge 12 *die Aprilis*	25
	Henrie Smithe, of Bisley 16 *die Aprilis* ...	25
	Thomas Warne, of Snowshill *eodem*	25
	Nicholas Sauckie, of the Cittie of Glouc. Gen. *eodem*	25
	Luke Garnaunce, of the same, Alderman *eodem die*	25
	Henrie Hazarde, of the same *eodem die* ...	25
	Henrie Whitinge, of Upton, Clothier *eodem* ...	25
	John Dennys, of Westerley, Gen. 18 *die Aprilis*	25
	George Foorde, of Puclechurche *eodem* ...	25
	Katheryn Huntley, of Froster, Vidua 19 *Aprilis*	25
	Robert Hale, of Wotton under Edge 20 *die Aprilis*	25
	Arthur Crew, of Wotton under Edge *eodem* ...	25
	Hugh Venne, of Synwell *eodem*	25
	James Doles, of Dowsborne, Gen. 21 *die Aprilis*	25
	Robert Partridge, of Cicester, Gen. *eodem* ...	25
	John Coxhall, of Cicester, Gen. *eodem*	25
	Robert Kyble, of Sowthroppe *eodem*	25
	Sir Gyles Pooles, Miles 22 *die Aprilis*	25
	John Blanchard, of Marchfield *eodem*	25
	Richard Webb, of the Cittie of Gloucester, Alderman *eodem* ... ... }	25
	Richard Coxe, of the same, Alderman *eodem die*	25
	James Clifford, of Frampton, Armiger 13 *Aprilis*	25
	Edward Badgeworth, of Presburie, Gen. 26 *Aprilis*	25
	George Badgeworth, of Presburie, Gen, 26 *Aprilis*	25
	John Bucke, of Biburie, Gen. 28 *Aprilis* ...	25
	Henrie Winchcombe, of Norlace, Gen. *eodem* ...	25
	John Litle, of the Cittie of Glouc. 29 *die Aprilis*	25
	John Baugh, of the same *eodem die*	25
	Laurence Singleton, of the Cittie of Gloucester, Alderman 30 *die* ... ... }	25
	William Fowler, of Stonehouse, Clothier *eodem*	25
May.	George Ligon, of Faireford, Gen. *primo die Maii*	25
	Elizabeth Robins, of Matson, Vidua *septimo de Maii* ... ... }	25
	John Cotton, of Wittington 10 *die Maii* ...	25
	Robert Rogers, of Wittington 16 *die Maii* ...	25
	William Selwyn, of Kingestanley *eodem* ...	25
	Matthew Crew, of Adderley, Clothier *eodem* ...	25

£

May.
Thomas Pirrey, of Synwell, Clothier *eodem* ... 25
Alexander Tenis, of Wickwarr, Clothier *eodem* 25
John Fettiplace, of Crowneallin, Gen. *ultimo die Maii* ... 25

June.
Robert Tailoe, of Strowde, Clothier *sexto die Junii* 25
Amicell Standford, of Stonehouse 13 *Junii* ... 25
James Bicke, of Naylesworth 14 *die Junii* ... 25
Richard Fowler, of Bisley *eodem* 25
Gyles Coxe, of Ablott's Court 16 *die Junii* ... 25
James Barrowe, of Hardwicke, Gen. 20 *die Junii* 25
William Atwood, of Beach *eodem die* 25
Robert Tibbott, of Winterburne *eodem* 50
Richard Clutterbuck, of Kingestanley 21 *of June* 25
William Clutterbuck, of Alkerton *eodem* ... 25
William Crompton, of Hartburie, Gen. 28 *Junii* 25
John Tailor, alias Cooke, of the Cittie of Glouc. *the* 11 *of June* 25

July.
Thomas Mason, of Hill *primo die Julii* ... 25
John Warkeman, of Lasbarough 8 *die Julii* ... 25
Richard Frigge, of Naylesworth *eodem* 25
*Symon Cotherington, of Cotherington, Armiger 24 *die Julii* 50
Henrie Cassy, of Wightfeild, Armiger 28 *die Julii* 25
Thomas Coxe, of Cleve, Gen. *ultimo die Julii* ... 25
*Rowland Atkinson, of the Citie of Glouc. 29 *Julii* 25
Arthur Baker, of Awste *ultimo die Julii* ... 25
Erasmus Prynne, of Awste *eodem* 25

August.
William Edmundes *the 5 of August* 25
Thomas Elkington *the 17* 25
Richard Allen 20 25
William Partridge 25 25
Richard Hill 31 25
John Wynyott *eodem* 25
William Hodges *eodem* 25
Richard Stevens *eodem* 25
James Stevens *eodem* 25

* Not charged.

		£.
Septemb.	Andrew Kettleby *the first of September* ...	25
	Richard Selwyn *eodem*	25
	William Trotman *eodem*	25
	Maurice Hardinge 12	25
	Ri. Poole 13	25
	Tho. Merritt *eodem*	25
	Richard Trotman *eodem*	25

HAMPSHIRE.

		£
Feb.	William Sendie, of Southampton, Gen. 23 *die Februarii*	25
	John Mercer of the same, Merchant *eodem die*	25
	Richard Bisenn, of the same *eodem* ...	25
	John Knight, of the same, Merchant ..	25
	Richard Kingesmill, of High Clere, Ar. 25 *Februarii*	50
	Frauncis Searle, of Cordered, Gen. 27 *die Februarii*	25
Marche.	Richard Whitehead, of West Titherley, *primo die Marcii*	25
	Willian Neale, of Warneford, Armiger *eodem*	50
	Richard Miller, of Amporte *secundo die Marcii*	50
	James Parkinson, of Exbury, Ar. *quarto die Marcii*	25
	Owen Totty, of Portesmouth *eodem die* ...	50
	Davie Bulbeck, of Southstonham 7 *die Marcii*	25
	William Bartholmew, of Midham, Gen. 8 *die Marcii*	25
	John Twine, of Woodmancote 9 *die Marcii*...	25
	William Hodson, of Winchester, Gen. 12 *die Marcii*	25
	Edward Goddarde, of Woodhey, Ar. *eodem* ...	50
	John Moulton, of Shamblehurst *eodem* ...	25
	Richard Cawes, Sen. of Upham, Gen. *eodem*	25
	Thomas Cutte, of Chilbolton, Ged. 13 *die Marcii*	25
	John Love, of Frexfield *eodem* ... ... ·	25
	Edward Cole, of Winchester, Gen. 14 *die Marcii*	25
	John Pittman, of Quarle 15 *die Marcii* ...	25
	Richard Brooke, of Whitchurche, Gen. 16 *dic Marcii*	25
	John Compton, of Petersfield, Gen. 24 *die Marcii*	25

£.

March.   Richard Goddard, of Southampton, Merchant, 24 }   25
       die Marcii }
       Roberte Godfrey, of Tichfeild, Gen.   25 *die Marcii*   25
       William Rickman, of Marchwood   27 *die Marcii*   50
       Robert Knaplake, of Southampton, Gen.   28 *die*
       Marcii   100
       John Langbrooke, of Mattingley, Gen.   *eodem*   25
       George Kingesmill, of Eanam, Ar.   29 *die Marcii*   25
       Robert White, of Aldershot, Ar.   *eodem*   ...   50
       Henrie Pinke, of Kempshott   *eodem*   ...   25
       William Jephson, of Troill, Ar.   *eodem*   ...   50
       Richard White, of Southwarnborowe, Armiger *eodem*   50

Aprill.   Henrie Florrye, of Hodham   *secundo die Aprilis*   25
       Nicholas Bacon, of Owlesburie, Gen.   *tercio die*   25
       William Badger, of Winchester   7 *die Aprilis*   50
       William Symondes, of Winchester   *eodem*   ...   50
       John Lyne, Jun. of Ringwood   7 *die Aprilis* ...   25
       Steven Tirrey, of Longe Sutton   8 *die Aprilis*   25
       Richard Strange, of Weston, Ar.   *eodem*   ...   25
       William Button, of Winchester   10 *die Aprilis*   25
       Gabriell White, of Charford, Arm.   *eodem*   ...   25
       Richard Pile, of Overwallopp   15 *die Aprilis*...   25
       John Marriner, of Portesdowne, Gen.   17 *Aprilis*   25
       John Padge, of Bentworth   20 *die Aprilis*   ...   25
       Richard Hardinge, of Hallyborne   *eodem*   ...   25
       John Merrett, of Altoun   *eodem*   25
       William Jamper, of Mylbrooke   21 *die Aprilis*   25
       Andrewe Pope, of Rockborne   *eodem*   ...   25
       William Peake, of Ashotte, Gen.   24 *die Aprilis*   100
       Henrie Carew, of Hordell, Ar.   *eodem*   ...   25
       James Hunt, of Popham   25 *die Aprilis*   ...   50
       Samuel Blackhouse, of Kingesley, Arm.   25 *Aprilis*   50
       Roger Hunt, of Luchfeild   28 *die Aprilis*   ...   25

Maye.   John Earlsman, of the Isle of Wight   *septimo die*
       Maii   50
       Thomas Hobson, of the same   *eodem*   ...   25
       John Lee, of the same   *eodem*   25
       Nicholas Wright, of Eastmeane   8 *die Maii* ...   25

B

		£.
Maye.	William Oglander, of the Isle of Wight, Gen. 14 *Maii*	50
	George Searle, of the same Ile *eodem die* ...	50
	Edward Richardes, of the same Ile *eodem* ...	50
	Anthonie Lisley, of the said Isle, Ar. *eodem*...	50
	John Curle, of the said Isle 7 *die Maii* ...	25
	Thomas Worsley, of the said Isle, Ar. 14 *die Maii*	50
	Thomas Urry, of the said Isle *eodem* ...	25
	John Jackman, of the said Isle *eodem* ...	25
	John Kingesmill, of Eaname, Ar. 9 *die Maii*	25
	Frauncis Odewaie, of Fordingbridge *eodem* ...	25
	Reynold Hanyton, of Bromley, Attorney 15 *Maii*	25
	Richard Kent, of Netherwallope *eodem* ...	25
	Michaell Knight, of Longard, in the Isle of Wight	25
	Richard Pregnish, of Pitt 21 *die Maii* ...	25
	Nicholas Venables, of Andever, Gen. 23 *die Maii*	25
	John Knight, of Chawton, Gen. 27 *die Maii*	50
	John Pescod, of Littleton, Gen. 29 *die Maii*	25
	Nicholas Mory, of Chawton 30 *die Maii* ...	25
June.	William Tulfe, of Avem *secundo die Junii* ...	25
	Robert Odber, of Hurne *eodem*	25
	Peter Woodford, of Newport, in the Ile of Wight *eodem*	25
	George Philpott, of Thruxton, Ar. 9 *Junii* ...	25
	Anthonie Barrowe, of Aven, Ar. 26 *Junii* ...	25
July.	Phillip Ogdeane, of Ellingham, Ar. *quinto Julii*	50
	William Watson, of Winchefeild, Gen. *eodem*	25
Septemb.	John Hoore, of Catrington 29 *die Septembris*	25
Octobris.	William Moore, of Tytherley 10 *die Octobris*	25
	John Edmondes, of Crawley 12 *die Octobris*...	25

HEREFFORD.

£.

Aprill. John Ballard, of Trebumfrey, alias Llanwarne 20 } 25
die Aprilis ... ...

Thomas Smaleman, Armiger 19 *die Aprilis*... 25

Maye. William Broome, of Broome 8 *die Maii* ... 25
William Bedford, of Chorlestree 9 *die Maii*... 25
Thomas Havard, of Willersley 12 *die Maii* ... 25
Richard Williams, of Monckburie Court *eodem* 25
Edward Gyles, of the Feild 13 *die Maii* ... 25
William Dansey, of Brynsopp *eodem* ... 25
William Jones, of Llanwarne- 22 *die Maii* ... 25
John Mainston, of Llangaran, alias Lanwarne
21 *Maii* ... ...: 25
Richard Darnell, of Castle Frome *eodem* ... 25
Edmonde Weaver, of Aymestree *eodem* ... 25
Thomas Trawter, of Otecroft 24 *die Maii* ... 25
John Weaver, of Stepleton, Armiger *eodem* ... 25
Richard Caple, of Bosburie 22 *die Maii* ... 25
Robert Aylwaie, Gen. 27 *die Maii* ... 25
Nicholas Garnons, of Morton, Armiger 28 *die Maii* 25
Hugh Smith, of Foxeley, Gen. 29 *die Maii*... 25
John Woolridge, of Dynmor, Gen. *eodem* ... 25
Charles Merrick, of Weston 16 *die Maii* ... 25

June. Martha Harford, Vidua *primo die Junii* ... 25
Anthonie Kirte, Armiger *eodem* 25
John Harpur *secundo die Junii* 25
Richard Barroll, of Bronsall *primo die Junii* 25
Richard Bromwich, of Heref. 6 *die Junii* ... 25
Thomas Webb, of Mounton 11 *die Junii* ... 25
James Ravenhill, of Woohope 19 *die Junii*... 25
Henrie Chippenham, of Brosemonde, Armiger
4 *Junii* 25
John Jones, of Putley 21 *die Junii* ... 25

August. Anthonie Washborne, Armiger 28 *die Augusti* 25
James Crofte, of Aymstre, Gen. 27 *die Augusti* 25
Fraunces Lovell, Armiger 28 *die Augusti* ... 25

		£.
October.	Richard Tompkins, of Mornington, Armiger *secundo die Octobris*	25
	Henrie Broie, of Ledburie 16 *die Octobris*	25
	John Collins, of Foie 18 *die Octobris*	25
	Thomas Chamber, of Litle Marcle *eodem*	25
	Roger Blunt, of Munckland 18 *die Octobris*	25
	Tho. Maylard, of Heref. 23 *die Octobris*	25
	John Lentall, of Burcott 27 *die Octobris*	25
	Edward Skynner, Clothier 30 *die Octobris*	25
Novemb.	William Bennett, of Heref. *tercio die Novembris*	25
	Richard Clement of Putteston *quarto die Novembris*	25
	Edward Rawlings of Herefford *eodem die*	25
	James Wilcox, of Herefford 9 *die Novembris*	25
	William Boyle, of Herefford 16 *die Novembris*	25
Decemb.	Thomas Serche, of Fairetree *quarto die Decembris*	25
	John Hayward, Gen. 12 *die Decembris*	25
	James Winton 1 *Decembris*	25

HERTFORD.

		£.
March.	George Knighton, Armiger *tercio die Marcii*	25
	Raphe Ratcliffe, Gen. *eodem*	25
	Ellzabeth Chune, Vidua *quarto die Marcii*	25
	William Beswicke, Gen. *eodem*	25
	William Sherwood *sexto die Marcii*	25
	Edward Biscoe, Jun. 10 *die Marcii*	25
	Marie Browne, Vidua *eodem*	25
	Thomas Parsons, Gen. *eodem die*	25
	John Gibbe, Gen. *eodem*	25
	Jane Bashe, Vidua *eodem*	25
	Thomas Turner, Yeoman *eodem*	25
	John Tarborowe, Armiger *eodem*	25
	Henrie Sadler, Armiger *eodem*	50
	Edward Fitz John 11 *die Marcii*	25
	Edward Bigge, Yeoman *eodem*	25

£.

March.
William Grubbe 12 *die Marcii* ...	...	25
Thomas Northe, Gen. 13 *die Marcii*	...	25
Roberte Hyde, Armiger *eodem* ...	...	50
John Clerke *eodem die* ...	...	25
Clement Manestye 14 *die Marcii* ...	...	25
Henrie Mayne 15 *die Marcii*	...	50
Robert Barbor 17 *die Marcii* ...	...	25
William Halsey *eodem die*	...	25
John Mitchell, Sen. 18 *die Marcii*..	...	25
Charles Nodes, Gen. *eodem* ...	...	25
Michaell Meade, Gen. *eodem* ...	...	50
George Clarke *eodem* ...	...	25
William Clerk *eodem* ...	...	25
Thomas Harmer *eodem* ...	..	25
George Graveley, Gen. 19 *die Marcii*	...	25
Thomas Chapman *eodem* ...	...	25
Henrie Spurlinge, Yeoman 20 *die Marcii*	...	25
Symonde Warren 22 *die Marcii* ...	...	25
George Feild 23 *die Marcii* ...	...	25
Robert Spencer, Armiger *eodem* ...	...	25
Robert Wolley, Gen. *eodem* ...	...	50
John Andrew, Sen. 24 *die Marcii* ...	...	25
John Binge, Gen. 29 *die Marcii* ...	...	25
William Ewer *eodem* ...	...	25
Thomas Ewer *eodem* ...	...	25
Thomas Gardiner *eodem* ...	...	25
Thomas Ansell 31 *daie of Marche* ...	...	25

Aprill.
Thomas Dermer *quinto die Aprilis*	...	25
Foulke Onslowe, Armiger *sexto die Aprilis*		50
William Crawley *eodem* ...	...	25
John Hurste *eodem* ...	...	25
Henrie Foster 13 *die Aprilis*	...	25
William Samme *eodem* ...	..	25
George Grave 14 *die Aprilis* ...	...	25
Robert Garnett 16 *die Aprilis* ...	...	25
Jo. Sutton, Gen. 18 *die Aprilis* ...	...	25
Edward Briscoe 29 *die Aprilis* ...	...	25
John Rooley 29 *die Aprilis* ...	...	25

		£.
Maye.	William Muffett, Gen. *secundo die Maii* ...	25
	Edward Newport, Armiger *eodem*... ` ...	50
	Andrew Gray, Armiger *tercio die Maii* ...	25
	George Chasey, Gen. *eodem*	25
	Richard Canfeild *sexto die Maii*	25
	Richard Smithe, Armiger 10 *die Maii* ...	50
	William Godfrey, alias Cowper, Gen. *eodem*...	25
	Rowland Bafford, Gen. 26 *die Maii* ...	25
	Wiiiiam Mayne *eodem*	25
	Stephen Nobbes 28 *die Maii*	25
	William Preston, Gen. 30 *die Maii* ...	25
	John Okston, Sen. *eodem*	25
Julye.	George Kimpton, Gen. 15 *die Julii* ...	25
	John Kent 29 *die Julii*...	25

HUNTINGDON.

		£.
Aprill.	Thomas Cordall *quinto die Aprilis* ...	25
	Thomas Daniell *sexto die Aprilis*	25
	John Bedells, Gen. *septimo die Aprilis* ...	50
	William Sarvington, Gen. *eodem*	25
	Thomas Saulter 8 *die Aprilis*	25
	Thomas Marsh, Gen. *eodem*	25
	John Pedley *eodem*	25
	Richard Godfrey 9 *die Aprilis*	25
	Johan Calton, Vidua *eodem*	25
	William Bedells, Gen. *eodem*	25
	Thomas Awder, Gen. 12 *die Aprilis* ...	25
	Henrie Newman *eodem*	25
	Robert Gylate *eodem*	25
	Kénelm Kent 18 *die Aprilis*	25
	Richard Draper *eodem die*	25
	John Palmer 29 *die Aprilis*	25
Maye.	Thomas Haell *primo die Maii*	25
	William Cony, Armiger *eodem*	25

			£.
Maye.	Michaell Beale *secundo die Maii* ...	...	25
	Anthonie Warde *septimo die Maii*	...	25
	Owen Biggs 16 *die Maii*	...	25
	John Cranwell *the* 18 *Maii*	...	25
June.	Robert Wells *septimo die Junii* ...	...	25

KENTT.

		£.
Feb.	John Toufton, of Hotfeild, Armiger 9 *die Februarii* ...,	100
	John Knell, of Bruckland 17 *die Februarii*...	50
	John Nutte, of Canterburie 18 *Februarii* ...	50
	Markes Bury, of Canterburie *eodem*	50
	William Hayward, of Hartic 24 *Februarii* ...	50
	John Fowle, of Hawkehurste *eodem*	25
	Henric Drayton, of Canterburie *eodem*	50
	Thomas Cleeve, of Preston 25 *dis Februarii*	100
March.	Richard Boys, of Hawkehurst, Gen. *primo die Marcii*	50
	Thomas Judgham, of Goodminston, Armiger *eodem*	25
	Richard Potman, of Stockburie *tercio die Marcii*	50
	Thomas Odierne, of Longbridg *eodem*	25
	Edward Warrham, of Wingham, Gen. *eodem*	50
	John Gookyn, of Norbone *eodem* ...	50
	Henric Oxney, of Wingham *eodem*	100
	John Taylor, of Willesborrowe, Gen. *eodem* ...	25
	William Tilden, of Wyllesborrowe *eodem*	25
	Henric Gibbon, of Rolvinden *quarto die Marcii*	50
	Richard Thornehill, of Bromley *sexto die Marcii*	100
	John Sidley, of Aylesford, Armiger *eodem*	50
	Edmonde Cooke, of Northraie, Gen. *eodem* ...	25
	Thomas Watton, of Addington, Armiger *eodem*	25
	John Rose, of Canterburie *eodem* ...	50
	Marten Barneham, of Hollingborne 7 *die Marcii*	50

£.

March. Anthonie Manie, of Linton, Gen. *eodem* ...	25
John Scott, of Bromley, Gen. *eodem* ...	25
Thomas Rheader, of Bredgare 10 *die Marcii*	50
Robert Binge, of Wrotham, Armiger *eodem*...	100
John Colson, of Raynham 11 *die Marcii* ...	50
Timothie Lowe, of Bromley, Gen. *eodem* ...	25
John Sea, of Herne 12 *die Marcii* ...	25
Humfrey Donnett, of Opington, Gen. 13 *Marcii*	25
John Smithe, of Crayford, Gen. 14 *die Marcii*	25
John Kinge, th'elder, of Cranebrooke *eodem*	50
Thomas Hawkins, of Boughton under Bleane, Gent. 15 *Marcii*	50
Leonard Cotton, of Canterburie *eodem* ...	50
Thomas Walker, of Fawkham 17 *die Marcii*	50
John Monncke, of Stone *eodem*	25
Thomas Brodnax, of Godmersham 18 *Marcii*	50
William Keyfar, of Hollingborne, Gen. 10 *Marcii*	50
John Hawle, of Willesborrowe 21 *die Marcii*	50
John Sharpe, of Westwell *eodem*	50
William Morbred, of Canterburie, Gen. 22 *Marcii*	50
Clement Finche, of Mylton, Gen. *eodem* ...	50
William Bixe, of Canterburie 27 *Marcii* ...	50
Thomas Sheffe, of Cranebrooke 28 *Marcii* ...	50
Anne Sidley, of Southfleete, Vidua 29 *Marcii*	100
Aprill. Gilbert Penny, of Canterburie, Alderman *primo Aprilis*	50
Lawrence Omer, of Staple 9 *Aprilis* ...	100
Robert Bargrave, of Bridge 15 *Aprilis* ...	50
John Leonard, of Knolle, Armiger 16 *Aprilis*	100
Thomas Linche, of Staple 17 *Aprilis* ...	50
Thomas Whetnall, of Asshe, Gen. *eodem* ...	50
John Harrison, of Caple *eodem*	50
William Blount, of Halden, Gen. *eodem* ...	50
William Brockman, of Newington, nere Heith 23 *Aprilis*	100
John Baker, th'elder, Armiger 24 *Aprilis* ...	50
Frauncis Culpepper, of Grenwaie Cort, Gen. 30 *Aprilis*	50

£

		£
May.	Valentine Norton, of Fordiche, Gen. *primo die Maii*	50
	Henrie Cutt *secundo die Maii*	50
	Gyles Ente, of Sandwich Denizon *tercico Maii*	100
	Sir Jo. Hawkins, of Detford, Miles *sexto die Maye*	100
	Reginald Knatchbull, of Saltwood, Gen. 7 *die Maii*	50
	William Silliard, of Stonbridg, Gen. 13 *die Maii*	50
	Sir John Rooper, of Lynsted, Miles 14 *die Maii*	50
	Thomas Payton, of Knolton, Armiger 18 *die Maii*	50
June.	Robert Spracklyn, of Thannet *quinto Junii*...	50
	Richard Hartie, of Gorende, in the Ile of Thannet *eodem*	50
	Thomas Denwoode, of Beakesborne *eodem* ...	25
	Mathew Mynnis, of Sandwich *sexto Junii* ...	50
	William Crayford, of Great Mongeham *septimo Junii*	50
	Thomas Harrendon, of Lydd *eodem* ...	50
	Thomas Dike, of Pembery, alias Pepinbury *eodem*	50
	John Stoke, th'elder, of Shepperdes Wold 10 *die Junii*	50
	Robert Honnywood, of Charinge, Arm. 12 *die Junii*	50
	Nicholas Myller, of Wrotham 13 *Junii* ...	50
	Thomas Rooper, of Eltham, Armiger 14 *Junii*	50
	Guy Wilmot, of Keith 17 *Junii*	25
	John Hales, of Tenterden. Gen. *eodem* ...	25
	Leonard Spracklyn, of Canterburie *eodem* ...	50
	Thomas Ploomer, of New Romney 18 *die Junii*	25
	Richard Huffman, of Esterie 19 *Junii* ...	25
	Thomas Barrham, of Teston, Gen. *eodem* ...	50
	Arnold Kinge, of Beckenham 20 *Junii* ...	50
	Thomas Fraunces, of Wickham Busshes 23 *Junii*	25
	Thomas Herdson, of Fowlkeston, Gen. *eodem*	100
July.	Thomas Godfrey, of Lidd 9 *die Julii* ...	100
	Edward Meryweather, of Shepperdes Weald 24 *Julii*	50
	Edward Pocdage, of Beakesborne 25 *of July*	25

F

			£.
August.	Thomas Fludde *the 20 of August*...	...	50
Septemb.	Henry Bosevile *the 20 of September*	...	100
October.	Peter Knight 9 *October*		25
	John Berry *the* 14		50
Novemb.	Thomas Pagett *the* 7 *November*		50
	William Southland 10		50
	William Bayneham 11		50
	Edward Eston 13		25
Jan.	John Norden 21 *Januar.*		50

LANCASTER.

			£.
March.	Edward Norres 16 *die Marcii*		25
	George Ireland *eodem die*		25
	Edward Scaresbeck, Armiger *eodem* ...		25
	James Worseley, Armiger *eodem*		25
	William Massye, Armiger *eodem*		25
	Henrie Bannester, Armiger *eodem* ...		25
	Barnabie Kitchen, Armiger *eodem* ...		25
	Richard Blundell, Armiger *eodem*... ...		25
	James Anderton, Armiger *eodem*		25
	Richard Bold, Armiger *eodem*		25
	Richard Mollineux, Armiger *eodem* ...		25
	John Cultheath, Armiger *eodem*		25
	Lawrence Ireland, Armiger *eodem* ...		25
	Thomas Lancaster, Armiger *eodem* ...		25
	Myles Gerrarde, Armiger *eodem*		25
	William More, Armiger *eodem*		25
	Adam Harden, Armiger *eodem*		25
	Thomas Standishe, Esq. *eodem*		25
	Sir Edmonde Trafforde, Miles 14 *die Marcii*		100
	Sir Jo. Radcliffe, Miles *eodem*		100
	Raphe Asheton, Armiger *eodem*		25
	Richard Hollande, Armiger *eodem* ...		25

£

Richard Asheton, Armiger *eodem*	25
James Asheton, Armiger *eodem*	25
Thomas Leigh, Armiger *eodem*	25
Christofer Anderton, Armiger *eodem* ...	50
George Lathon, Gen. *eodem*	25
Edward Brewerton, Armiger *eodem* ...	25
Humfrey Houghton, Gen. *eodem*	25
Richard Tipping, Gen. *eodem*	25
Giles Hilton, Gen. *eodem*	25
Robert Heskeith, Armiger *eodem*	50
Edward Standishe, Armiger *eodem* ...	50
John Fletewood, Armiger *eodem*	50
Serjant Walmesly, Gen. *eodem*	25
Robert Charnocke, Armiger *eodem* ...	25
Henrie Eccleston, Armiger *eodem*... ...	25
Richard Brewerton, Armiger *eodem* ...	25
John Cowerden, Gen. *eodem*	25
Roger Diconson *eodem*	25
Thomas Clayton *eodem*	25
Richard Worseley *eodem*	25
William Farrington, Armiger *eodem* ...	25
Sir John Southworth, Miles 20 *die Marcii*...	25
Nicholas Banester, Armiger *eodem* ...	25
Edward Osbaldston, Armiger *eodem* ...	25
Roger Nowell, Armiger *eodem*	25
Richard Walmesly, Gen. *eodem*	25
John Talbot *eodem*	25
John Lowe *eodem*	25
Serjant Shutleworth 16 *die Marcii* ...	25
John Dewhurst 20 *die Marcii*	25
Thomas Houghton, Armiger *eodem* ...	100
*Henrie Butler, Armiger *eodem*	25
*John Singleton, Armiger *eodem*	25
*Thomas Eccleston, Armiger *eodem* ...	25
Thomas Preston, Armiger *eodem*	50
Christopher Preston, Armiger *eodem* ...	25
William Fleminge, Armiger *eodem* ...	25
John Bradley, Armiger *eodem*	25

* Not charged.

			£.
March.	George Midleton, Armiger *eodem*...	...	25
	William Crofte, Armiger *eodem* ...	...	25
	*Robert Bindlowes *eodem* ...	...	25
	*William Thorneborough, Armiger *eodem*	...	25
Aprill.	*John Westbie, Armiger 26 *Aprilis*	...	25
	*Roger Breers, Armiger *eodem* ...	...	25
June.	*John Byrom, Armiger 24 *Junii* ...	...	25

LEICESTER.

			£.
	Frauncis Beomount, Armiger 24 *Aprilis*	...	25
	John Stanford, Gracier 29 *Aprilis*...	...	25
Maye.	Richard Paramor, Armiger *sexto die Maii*	...	25
	Valentyne Hartopp, Gen. 11 *die Maii*	...	25
	Bryan Cave, Armiger 12 *die Maii*	...	25
	Richard Walker 14 *die Maii* ...	...	25
	Robert Brookesby, Armiger 16 *die Maii*	...	25
	Richard Evington 25 *die Maii* ...	...	25
	Frauncis Smithe, Armiger 27 *die Maii*	...	25
	Ralphe Whaley, Gen. *eodem* ...	...	25
	George Ashebye, Armiger 28 *die Maii*	...	25
June.	William Digby, Armiger 10 *die Junii*	...	25
	John Tomworth, Armiger 12 *Junii*	...	25
	Edwarde Turvile, Armiger 14 *Julii*	...	25
	William Blunt, Armiger 16 *Junii*	...	25
	Edward Pell 16 *die Junii* ...	...	25
	Stephen Rogers, Gen. 20 *Junii* ...	...	25
	Frauncis Sherard, Armiger 24 *Junii*	...	25
	Edward Pate, Armiger 28 *Junii* ...	...	25
July.	William Lawe, Gen. *quarto Julii* ...	...	25
	Mawrice Barkie, Arm. 14 *Julii* ...	...	25

*Not charged.

		£
August.	Frasmus Smithe 9 *August*	25
Septemb.	Robert Hasilwoode 2 *Septembris*	25
	William Roberts 6	25
	John Elkington 8	25
	John Copeland 10	25
	Basil Brooke *eodem*	25
	Roberte Kilbie *eodem*	25
	Mitchaell Cosen 19	25
	Edmunde Temple 25	25
	Nicholas Perpointe 27	25
	Thomas Walronde 28	25
	John Plumbe 29	25
October.	Richard Brocke 12 *Octobris*	25
	Richard Kestyn *the* 23	25
	John Grever 25	25
	William Johnson 27	25
	John None 28...	25
	Thomas Lanye 30	25
Novemb.	Jane Bowes, Widow 3 *Novembris*	25
	William Coke 14	25

LINCOLN.

	£.
Roberte Carr, of Sleeford, Armiger 22 *die Aprilis*	100
George St. Poole, Armiger 26 *die Aprilis* ...	50
William Hamby, of Tatchwell 9 *Aprilis* ...	50
John South, of Kelby *eodem*	50
Nicholas Thornedike, of Grenefeld *eodem* ...	50
Francis Copledike, of Harrington *eodem* ...	50
Roberte Grantham, of Dunham 21 *Aprilis* ...	50
Thomas Tailor, of Lincolne 9 *Aprilis* ...	50
Frauncis Tompson, of Boothby 22 *Aprilis* ...	25
John Frye, of Colby 9 *Aprilis*	25
Anthonie Newlove, of Helpringham 22 *Aprilis*	25
Robert Barber, of Haubeck in Wellesforth *eodem*	25

	£.
Richard Pell, of Credington *eodem* ...	25
Thomas Lister, of Sudbrooke *eodem* ...	25
William Callis, of Litle Hawle *eodem* ..	25
Robert Cammok, of Sleeford *eodem* ...	25
Bartolomew Armyn, of Osgardby *eodem* ...	25
Robert Cholmley, of Burton 12 *Aprilis* ...	25
George Wyat of Barrowby 12 *Aprilis* ...	25
John Martyn, of Allyngton *eodem* ...	25
Thomas Beetson, of Swarby 22 *Aprilis* ...	25
Richard Black, of Roppesly *eodem* ...	25
Robert Carr, of Gedney, Armiger *eodem* ...	25
Edmunde Brimston, of Moulton *eodem* ...	25
William Stowe, of Holbiche *eodem* ...	25
Thomas Fisher, of Gedney *eodem*	25
William Davison, of Weston *eodem* ...	25
George Hall, of Sutton *eodem*	25
John Gambling, of Spalding *eodem* ...	25
Thomas Howson, of Wigtoft *eodem* ...	25
Richard Ormshead, of Quadring *eodem* ...	25
John Lockton, of Swynshead *eodem* ...	25
Giles Bogg, of Sutterton *eodem*	25
William Whittingham, of Sutterton *eodem* ...	25
William Harryman, of Donington *eodem* ...	25
Thomas Harryman, of Quadringe *eodem* ...	25
Thomas Harvey, of Kirton *eodem*	25
William Feelde, of Wilberton *eodem* ...	25
Frauncis Reade, of Wrangle *eodem* ...	25
John Feelde, of Benington *eodem*	25
William Tindall, of Boston *eodem*	25
John Gawdrie, of Boston *eodem*	25
Thomas Orsbye, of Boston *eodem*	25
Richard Draper, of Boston 12 *Aprilis* ...	25
Thomas Margery, of Boston 22 *Aprilis* ...	25
Nicholas Saunderson, of Fillingham 9 *Aprilis*	25
Charles Dymmock, of Cotes 9 *Aprilis* ...	25
Anthonie Sultill, of Redborne *eodem* ...	25
Andrew Gedney, of Bagg Enderby *eodem* ...	25
John Jon, of Barrowe *eodem*	25
Edward Goodrick, of East Kirkbie 22 *Aprilis*	25
Edward Marburie, of Gersbye 9 *Aprilis* ...	25

	£.
Symon Wolbye, of Burgh *eodem*	25
James Balder, of Sutton 22 *die Aprilis* ...	25
Thomas Hansert, of Wickenly 20 *die Aprilis*	25
John Stanley, of Stickford 9 *Aprilis* ...	25
John Blauncherde, of Lowthe *eodem* ...	25
William Patrick, of East Rayson *eodem* ...	25
Edward Maddison, juxta Castor *eodem* ...	25
Anthonie Edmonde, of Sutton 22 *die Aprilis*	25
John Hobson, of Spaldinge *eodem*... ...	25
John Caiter, of Markett Rayson 9 *Aprilis* ...	25
Vincent Welby, of Thorpe *eodem*	25
George Skipwith, of Cottam 16 *Aprilis* ...	25
John Wetherwick, of Claxby 9 *Aprilis* ...	25
Edward Nutt, of Yarborough *eodem* ...	25
Nicholas Girlington, of Normanby 12 *Aprilis*	25
Oliver Kennythorpe, of Carleton Parva 9 *Aprilis*	25
Richard Rosseter, of Sommerby *eodem* ...	25
Edward Skearne, of Bonby 18 *Aprilis* ...	25
Thomas Ellis, of Wyham 9 *die Aprilis* ...	25
William Fitzwilliam, of Maplethorpe *eodem*. .	25
Robert Beach, alias Leach, of Belchworth *eodem*	25
Thomas Copledike, of Lusbie *eodem* ...	25
John Baylie, of Normanbye 12 *Aprilis* ...	25
Andrew Eastwood, of Roughton 9 *Aprilis* ...	25
Roberte Phillippes, of Wispington *eodem* ...	25
Marmaduke Tirwhit, of Skotter 9 *Aprilis* ...	25
Robert Shadforth, of Gainsborrow 14 *Aprilis*	25
George Farmery, of Northorpe 9 *Aprilis* ...	25
John Popple, of Dalderby *eodem*	25
Leonard Esterby, of Halton *eodem* ...	25
Henrie Lyon, of Warton *eodem*	25
Edward Tirwhitt, of Steynfeild *eodem* ...	25
William Lunne, of Apley *eodem*	25
John Litleburie, of Staynesbye *eodem* ...	25
Vincent Welbye, of Hawstead *eodem* ...	25
Thomas Litleburie, of Staynesbye *eodem* ...	25
John Neale, of Hornccastle *eodem* ...	25
Edward Overy, of Toynton 9 *Aprilis* ...	25
Vincent Folnebye, of Foneby 9 *Aprilis* ...	25
Nicholas Saunderson, of Reasby *eodem* ...	25

£

Robert Smithe, of Horsington   *eodem*   ..   25
William Hennage, of Benington   20 *Aprilis* ...   25
Edmond Yarbrough. of Lincoln   9 *Aprilis* ...   25
William Knight, of Lincolne   *eodem*   ...   25
John Wymerk, of Gretford   *eodem*...   ...   25
Symon Hareby, of Thurleby   *eodem*   ...   25
William Barker, of Uffington   *eodem*   ...   25
Robert Beevar, of Longtoft   *eodem*...   ...   25
Thomas Barber, of Dembleby   *eodem*   ...   25

May.   Edward Heron, of Stamford   *primo die Maii*   25

Aprill.   Sir George Henadge, Miles   20 *Aprilis*   ...   50
Sir John Mounson, Miles   9 *Aprilis*   ...   50
John Savile, of Addington   *eodem*   50

May.   William Revitt, of Rowleston   *primo die Maii*   25
Charles Husse, of Lynwood   *eodem*   ...   50
Anthonie Irebye, of Whapleade   *eodem*   ...   25
Richard Bowles, of Boston   *eodem*   50
Edmonde Hall, of Gretford   *eodem*   ...   25
Thomas Conye, of Bassingthorpe   *eodem*   ...   100
Christofer Berisford, of Ledenham   *eodem*   ...   25
John Broxholme, of Otbye   20 *Maii*   ...   25
Roger Gregory, of Stockwith   *eodem*   ...   25
Symon Walcott, of Swaton   *eodem*...   ..   25

MIDDLESEX.

£.

Feb.   Martin James, Register of the Chauncery   9
Februarii   50
Humfrey Smithe, One of the Iudges of the }
Sherifs Cort in London...   ...   }   50
Thomas Fowler, of St. Martins in the Fields
12 *Februarii*   25
Edmonde Standen, of Chauncery Lane   *eodem*   50
Richard Garth, One of the Clarks of the Petti-
bagg   *eodem*   50

£.

		£.
Feb.	Thomas Fermore, of Clarkenwell, Gen. 13 *Februarii*	25
	Robert Peter, of Westminster, Armiger *eodem*	50
	Richard Warren, of Mylcande, Armiger 14 *Februarii*	100
	Edmond Downinge, of High Holborn, Gen. *eodem*	25
	Stephen Vaughan, of Norton Folgate 16 *Februarii*	25
	Raphe Rookeby, Armiger, of St. Katherine's 17 *die Feb.*	30
	John Fisher, of Westminster, Baker *eodem* ...	25
	Robert Atkinson, of Chauncery, Lane Armiger *eodem*	25
	Henrie Walronde, Armiger *eodem* ...	25
	Thomas Harby, of Hillingdon, Armiger 18 *die Februarii*	25
	John Barne, of Wilsdon, Armiger 19 *Feburarii*	30
	Sir John Arundell, of Clerkenwell, Knight *eodem*	50
	John Towneley, of Enfield, Armiger *eodem* ...	25
	John Manchell, of Hackney, Armiger 20 *Februarii*	30
	Sir John Tresham, of Hoggesdon, Miles 21 *Februarii*	50
	Jo. Hawtrey, of Ruislipp, Armiger 22 *Februarii*	25
	Thomas Wilmott, of Chauncerie Lane, Gen. *eodem*	25
	William Drew, one of th'exigenters of London 24 *Feb.*	25
	Thomas Crompton 26 *Februarii*	50
	John Page, of Wemley 28 *die Februarii* ...	25
March.	William Hopkins, of the Tower *primo die Marcii*	25
	Elizabeth Scorye, of Hallywell Street, Vidua *secundo Marcii*	25
	William Stidolph, of St. Gyles in the Feild, Gen. *eodem*	25
	Frauncis Vaughan, of Littleton, Arm. *quarto die Marcii*	25
	John Francklyn, of Cannons *sexto die Marcii*	30
	William Dalby, of Tattenham, Gen. 11 *Marcii*	25
	Robert Nicoll, of Mylles Pitt 14 *die Marcii*...	25
	Henric Marche, of Greneford *eodem* ...	25
	Ambrose Coppinger, of Stanwell, Armiger *eodem*	25

		£.
March.	William Bowes, of St. John Street, Gen. 28 *Marcii*	25
	Jo. Colbrand, of St. Martins in the Feilde *eodem*	25
	William Muschampe, of Kensington, Gen. 29 *Marcii*	40
	Richard Peacock, of Finchcley, Armiger 12 *Marcii*	50
Aprill.	Thomas Audeley, of Hackney, Gen. 23 *Aprilis*	25
	Anthonie Brigge, alias Bridge, of Tuttlestreat 15 *Aprilis*	25
Maye.	Anthonie Millington, of the Strande, Gen. *sexto Maii*	25
	Derrick Heldinge, of St. Martins in the Feild 7 *die Maii*	25
	Thomas Lucas, of Bednoll Grene, Gen *eodem*	25
	Thomas Cowper, of Westminster 12 *die Maii*	25
	Roberte Wilkes. of Islington, Brewer 25 *die Maie*	30
	William Kimpton, of Hadley, Armiger 17 *die Maii*	50
	Edward Cordall, One of the six Clerks, Armiger 28 *die Maii*	30
	William Curle, of Enfield *eodem*	25
	George Mackworth, of Harnesey, Armiger 29 *Maii*	30
	John Fuller, Armiger 28 *die Maii* ...	50
June	Andrew Mallorie, of Tottenham, Armiger 10 *Junii*	25
	William Burrowes, of Lymehouse, Armiger 11 *Junii*	25
	John Povye, of Fryarne Barnett, Gen. 12 *Junii*	25
	Roger Daie, of Drayton, Gen. 28 *Junii* ...	25
July	Thomas Arnewaie, of Westminster *secundo Julii*	25
	Ladie Gresham, of Austerley, Vidua 11 *Julii*	100

NORFFOLK.

			£.
Aprill.	Ambrose Fiske *sexto die Aprilis* ...	...	25
	Thomas Butt, Armiger 8 *die Aprilis*	...	25
	Vincent Carr 9 *die Aprilis* ...	...	25
	William Gassington *eodem* ...	...	25
	Edmond Framyngham *eodem* ...	...	25
	John Kinge *decimo die Aprilis* ...	...	25
	Andrew Thetford *eodem*... ...	...	25
	Sir William Paston, Miles 11 *Aprilis*	...	50
	Edward Paston *eodem*	...	50
	Marie Paston *eodem*	...	25
	Thomas Grosse *eodem*	...	25
	John Hubberd *eodem*	...	25
	William Rugg *eodem*	...	50
	Hammound Claxon	..	25
	Robert Kempe *eodem*	...	25
	Robert Reade *eodem*	...	25
	Richard Baker 12 *Aprilis* ...	...	50
	Humfrey Guybon *eodem*... ...	...	25
	John Pagrave *eodem*	...	40
	Martyn Barney *eodem*	...	25
	James Athill *eodem*	..	25
	John Wright 13 *die Aprilis* ...	...	25
	Thomas Barrowe *eodem*	...	50
	Henrie Russell 14 *die Aprilis* ...	...	25
	Robert Tylney 15 *Aprilis* ...	...	25
	William Armiger 20 *die Aprilis* ...	...	25
	Charles Cornewallis 22 *Aprilis* ...	...	50
	Henrie Toll 23 *die Aprilis* ...	...	25
	Robert Pagrave *eodem*	...	25
	Richard Allen *eodem*	...	25
	Richard Kett *eodem*	...	25
	Robert Downes, of Bodney *eodem*...	...	25
	William Fenn *eodem*	...	50
	Ellen Stallen *eodem*	...	25
	William Hart 24 *die Aprilis* ...	...	50
	Roberte Bedingfield *eodem* ...	...	50
	Anthonie Marker *eodem*... ...	..	25
	Slr Roberte Wood, Miles *eodem* ...	...	50
	Thomas Claborne 25 *die Aprilis* ...	...	25

			£.
Aprill.	Katherin Grave, Vidua *eodem*		100
	Thomas Gryme *eodem* ... ... ` ...		25
	Thomas Dey *eodem*		25
	Robert Futter *eodem*		25
	Henrie Kendall *eodem*		25
	William Cappes *eodem*		25
	Thomas Wright *eodem*		25
	Thomas Whipple *eodem*...		25
	William Cobbes *ultimo die Aprilis* ...		25
	Eustace Rolfe 12 *Aprilis*		25
Maye.	Richard Fisher *primo die Maii*		40
	William Blomefeild *eodem*		25
	Henrie Hawe *eodem*		25
	Gregorie Pratt *eodem*		25
	Thomas Baddescroft *secundo die Maii* ...		25
	Symon Cannon *eodem*		25
	Thomas Gleane *eodem*		25
	Thomas Layer *eodem*		25
	Christofer Layer *eodem*		25
	William Johnson *eodem*...		25
	Symon Bowde, Maior of the Citie of Norwich *eodem*		25
	Richard Whale *eodem*		25
	Christofer Zome *tercio die Maii*		25
	Thomas Pie *eodem*		25
	Thomas Peck *eodem*		25
	Anthonie Warner *eodem*		25
	Frauncis Rugg *eodem*		25
	Richard Beckham *eodem*		25
	William Porrye *eodem*		25
	Richard Jenkinson *eodem*		25
	Robert Hargitt *eodem*		25
	James Hubbard *eodem*		25
	Thomas Hearing *eodem*		25
	Bennet Cubitt *quinto die Maii*		25
	John Bartilmew *eodem*		25
	John Grosse *eodem*		25
	Roger Drewrie *eodem*		25
	Christofer Barrett *eodem*		**25**

			£.
Maye.	Henrie Davie *eodem*	25
	John Sucklinge *eodem*	25
	Clement Hirne 23 *die Maii*	25
	Thomas Pettus *eodem*	25
	George Bowgen *iodem*	25
	Richard Hatton *eodem*	25
	Richard Gresham *eodem*...	25
	Robert Basepole *eodem*	25
	Thomas Bedingfeild *secundo die Maii* ...	50
	Richard Barney *eodem*	25
	William Denny *eodem*	25
	John Castle *eodem*	25
	John Wiett 24 *die Maii*	25
	Robert Rogers *eodem*	25
	Alice Barney *eodem*	25
	Thomas Hicks *eodem*	25
	Anthonie Drurie *eodem*	25
	Richard Lovedaie *eodem*...	25
	Robert Ringwood *eodem*...	25
	Thomas Might 11 *die Maii*	25
	Richard Farror 24 *die Maii*	25
	Humfrey Rant *eodem*	25
	Thomas Stokes *eodem*	25
	John Elwyn *eodem*	25
	Peter Peterson *eodem*	25
	Thomas Secker *eodem*	25
	Walter Pike *eodem*	25
	Alexander Thurston 25 *die Maii*	25
	Gregorie Houlton *eodem*	25
	Robert Sucklinge *eodem*...	25
	Edward Johnson *eodem*	25
	Robert Prentice 30 *die Maii*	25
	John Aldhin, *eodem*	25
	Henrie Jerningham *eodem*	50
	Nicholas Daunock *eodem*	25
	Richard Hovell *eodem*	25
	John Sheringe *eodem*	25
	Robert Yarham *eodem*	25
	Lawrence Watts *eodem*	25
	Randall Smithe 29 *die Maii*	25

Maye.	Charles Waldgrave *ultimo die Maii*	...		50
	Stephen Upcrofte *eodem*	...	...	25
June.	Thomas Lovell 24 *die Junii*	...	...	50
	Nicholas Hore *sexto die Junii*	...	...	50
	Roger Buller 9 *die Junii*	...	...	25
	William Hudson 16 *die Junii*	...	...	25
	Richard Mason 23 *die Junii*	...	...	25
	John Davey 24 *die Junii*	...	...	25
	Robert Guybson *eodem* ...	...	...	25
	Thomas Lynford *eodem* ...	...	...	25
	Robert Beales *ultimo die Junii*	...	...	25
	William Roberte 9 *die Junii*	...	...	100
	Thomas Thursby 23 *die Junii*	...	...	50
July.	Thomas Knevitt 9 *die Julii*	...	...	25
	Thomas Husbonde 9 *die Julii*	...	...	25
	William Gaybon *eodem* ...	...	...	25
	John Sylver *eodem*	...	...	25
	Jeffry Might 14 *die Junii*	...	...	25
May.	Austen Whalley 2 *Maii*...		...	25
	Christofer Horne 23	...	...	25
June.	John Steward 10 *Junii*...	...	...	50
	Richard Stone 16	...	...	25
	John Kempesche 10	...	...	25
July.	Roberte Anstie 9 *Julye*...			25
August.	William Gybson *the first of August*		...	25
	William Parke 6	...	...	25
	John Willougbye 7	...	...	25
	Roberte Browne *eodem* ...	...	...	25
	Brian Harper 8	...	...	25
	Thomas Sponer 11	...	...	25
	Phillip Audeley 14	...	...	25
	Richard Basepole 21	...	...	25
March.	Cutbert Brereton 11 *Marcii*	...	...	25
	Frauncis Moundeford *eodem*	...	...	25

NORTHAMPTON.

		£.
Feb.	Edward Watson 17 *die Februarii*	25
March.	Thomas Tresham *secundo die Marcii* ...	25
	Martyn Wright *tercio die Marcii*	25
	Thomas Martyn *quinto die Marcii* ...	50
	Augustine Crispe *sexto die Marcii* ...	25
	Edmunde Elmes 1 *die Marcii*	50
	John Fraunces 12 *die Marcii*	50
	William Hicklyn 14 *die Marcii*	25
	Thomas Moone 18 *die Marcii*	25
	William Samwell *eodem*	25
	Robert Pargitor *eodem*	25
	John Stafford 19 *die Marcii* ·	50
	George Lynne *eodem*	50
	Johan Shugborow, *Vidua eodem*	25
	Edward Dudley *eodem*	25
	Arthur Brooke 20 *die Marcii*	25
	Thobie Chancie 22 *die Marcii* ...	50
	Thomas Maydwell 23 *die Marcii*	25
	Owen Rudgdale 28 *die Marcii*	25
	William Trust *eodem*	25
	Albon Butler *eodem*	25
	William Hughes *eodem*	25
Aprill.	Thomas Kirton 9 *die Aprilis* ...	50
	Henrie Pratt 14 *die Aprilis* ...	25
	George Sherley 12 *die Aprilis* ...	50
	Anthonie Jenkinson 20 *die Apriiis*	50
	John Brudnell 26 *die Aprilis* ...	50
Maye.	John Isham *secundo die Maii*	25
	John Freeman 7 *die Maii*	50
	Robert Osborne *eodem*	25
	Roger Charnocke 26 *die Maii* .. .. ·	25
	Leonard Barker *eodem*	25
	William Saunders *eodem*	50
	John Murden *eodem*	25
	Edward Haselrigg *eodem*	25
	Gilbert Pickeringe 30 *die Maii*	25

£.

		£.
Maye.	William Baldwyn *eodem*	25
	John Wake *eodem*	25
	Richard Worseley *eodem*	25
	Robert Matthew *ultimo die Maii*	25
June.	John Reade *primo die Junii* ...	25
	Robert Manley *eodem*	25
	Ambrose Agarde *eodem*	25
	William Lambe *tercio die Junii* ...	25
	Thomas Hacke *eodem*	50
	Erasmus Dredon *eodem*	50
	William Kinsman *quinto die Junii*	25
	John Kirkland *septimo die Junii* ...	25
	Robert Wingfeild 9 *die Junii* ...	25
	John Heward *eodem*	25
	Samuel Danvers 11 *die Junii* ...	25
	Stephen Harvey 12 *die Junii* ...	25
	Thomas Croswell 13 *die Junii* ...	25
	John Hensman *eodem*	25
	John Mercer *eodem*	25
	George Poulton 17 *die Junii* ...	25
	Frauncis Ashbye 18 *die Junii* ...	50
	John Bryan 27 *die Junii* ...	25
	William Margetts 26 *die Junii* ...	25
	John Neale 27 *die Junii* ...	50
July.	James Cleypole *primo die Julii* ...	50
	Robert Tredwaic 12 *die Julii* ...	25
	James Kendricke 20 *die Julii* ...	25
August.	Matthew Robinson 8 *August* ...	25

NOTTINGHAM.

		£.
March.	Sir Thomas Stanhopp, Miles *septimo die Marcii*	50
	The Ladie Winefride, Clifton 17 *die Marcii*...	50
	John Booth, of Grimley, Gen. 18 *die Marcii*	25

£.

		£.
March.	Nicholas Hamerton, of North Leverton, Gen. 17 *die Marcii*	25
	John Thorney, of Fenton, Armiger 18 *die Marcii*	25
	Peter Gelstopp, of Whatton, Gen. 18 *die Marcii*	25
	Robert Palmer, of Coulston Bassett *eodem* ...	25
	William Midleton, of Wauslowe 19 *die Marcii*	25
	Richard Hauley, of Wylforth, Gen. 21 *die Marcii*	25
	Edward Burnell, of Southwell, Gen. 25 *die Marcii*	25
	William Cardinall, of Egmonton, Arm. 28 *die Marcii*	25
	Henrie Pierpointe, Armiger 31 *die Marcii* ...	25
	Robert March, Maior of Nottingham *eodem* ...	25
Aprill.	Gregorie Walker, of Maunsfield, Gen. *primo die Aprilis*	25
	Richard Owtrom, of Carcolston, Gen. *eodem*	25
	William Brune, alias Gerves, of Estbridgford, Gen. *secundo Aprilis*	} 25
	Peter Rose, of Laxton, Armiger *tercio die Aprilis*	25
	Edward North, of Walkeringham, Gen. *eodem*	25
	Gerves Nevell, of Blythe, Gen. *eodem* ...	25
	Frauncis Brooxbye, of Staunton, Gen. *eodem*	25
	Nicholas Needam, of Kynalton, Gen. *eodem*	25
	Robert Bulbye, of Carcolston, Gen. *eodem* ...	25
	Humfrey Bonner, of Nott, Gen. *eodem* ...	25
	John Brownlowe, of Nott, Gen. *eodem* ...	25
	Thomas Markham, Armig. *quarto die Aprilis*	25
	William Kaye, of Newarke, Gen. *eodem* ...	25
Aprill.	John Elson, of Elson, Gen. *eodem*... ...	25
March.	Edward Burnell, of Sibthorp 31 *die Marcii*...	25
Aprill.	Christofer Newcombe, of Balderton *quarto Aprilis*	25
	Adam Arnall, of Elson *eodem*	25
	William Sutton, of Aram, Ar. *eodem* ...	25
	Richard Goston, of Tuxford, Gen. *eodem* ...	25
	Thomas Sturton, of Sturton, Gen. *eodem* ...	25

H

£.

Aprill.	Alexander Sampson, of South Leverton, Gen. *eodem*	25
	William Jessop, of Osbaston, Gen. *eodem* ...	50
	William Pocklington, of Scarle, Gen. *eodem*...	25
	John Addingsalls, of Epston, Gen. *quinto die Aprilis*	25
	Sir Anthonie Strelley, Miles *sexto die Aprilis*	25
	Edward Robinson, of Southwell, Gen. *eodem*	25
	John Teverey, of Stapleford, Gen. *septimo Aprilis*	25
	Sir Frauncis Willoughbie, Knight. 8 *die Aprilis*	50
	Lawrence Newton, of Kirkeby, Gen. 11 *die Aprilis*	25
	George Barwell, of Walkeringham, Gen. 14 *Aprilis*	25
	Sir William Hollis, Miles 23 *die Aprilis* ...	50
May.	Richard Whitmore, of Caunton, Gen. 25 *die Maii*	25
June.	William Staunton, of Staunton, Gen. 15 *die Junii*	25
July.	William Pendock, of Tollerton, Gen. *secundo die Julii*	25
	John Savell, of Oxton, Gen. 7 *die Julii* ...	25
	Thomas Hutchenson, of Awthorpe, Gen. *eodem*	25
	M. Stapleton, of Kempstoun 8 *die Julii* ..	25

OXON.

£.

Feb.	William Palmer, Gen. 21 *die Februarii* ...	50
	Raphe Spier *ultimo die Februarii*... ..	25
	John Whitton *eodem*	25
	Thomas Parsons *eodem*	25
March.	John Hartely *tercio die Marcii*	25
	Richard Spier *quarto die Marcii*	25
	Mr. Sheriffe *eodem*	25

£.

Murch.	Richard Dunt *quin'o die Marcii*	25
	Thomas Yate *eodem*	25
	The Ladie Hungerford *sexto die Marcii* ...	25
	William More *eodem*	25
	Robert Townesende *septimo die Marcii* ...	25
	Wylliam Shepperd *eodem*	25
	Walter Floyd 8 *die Marcii*	25
	Richard Lybbe 9 *die Marcii*	50
	Johan Heaster 10 *die Marcii*	25
	Anthonie Mollins *eodem*...	25
	John Symons *eodem*	25
	James Yate *eodem*	25
	William Napper 13 *die Marcii*	25
	Richard Lyde, alias Joyner 14 *die Marcii* ...	25
	Thomas Ashcombe 18 *die Marcii*... ...	25
	Nicholas Sawyer 19 *die Marcii*	25
	William Bustard *eodem*...	25
	Anthonie Elmes 20 *die Marcii*	25
Aprill.	Thomas Tipping *secundo die Aprilis* ...	50
	Frauncis Stonor *tercio die Aprilis* ...	25
	John Basten *quinto die Aprilis*	25
	Stephen Smithe *eodem*	25
	Thomas Teysdale 8 *die Aprilis*	25
	Henrie Samborne 10 *die Aprilis*	25
	Richard Fittzhew 11 *die Aprilis*	25
	Edmunde Hutchins 14 *die Aprilis* ...	25
	Thomas Clemens 21 *die Aprilis*	25
	Thomas Cotsford 24 *die Aprilis*	25
	Richard Raves *eodem*	25
May.	Michaell Chadwell, *primo die Maii*... ...	25
	John Marten *secundo die Maii*	25
	George Gough 14 *die Maii*	25
	Marie Barton 21 *die Maii*	25
	John Warner 27 *die Maii*	25
	Michaell Blunt Gen. 27 *die Maii* ...	50
	Robert Chamberlyn *quinto die Maii* ...	50
July.	John Williamson *secundo die Julii*	25

			£
July.	Steven Bryce *tercio die Julii* ...	...	25
	Robert Williamson 26 *die Julii* ...	. ...	25
October.	John Bowyer *the* 30 *of October* ...	...	25
Novemb.	James Maynerd 29 *Novembris* ...	...	25
	Bradshawe, Vidua *eodem*	...	25

RUTLAND.

			£
Maye.	Frauncis Palmes 12 *die Maii* ...	...	25
Julye.	Sir Andrew Nooell 20 *die Julii* ...	...	50
	Kenellm Digbye, Gen. *eodem* ...	...	50
	Roger Smithe, Gen. *eodem* ...	...	25
	John Hunt, Gen. *eodem*... ...	...	25
	Henry Herenden, Gen. *eodem* ...	...	25
	Anthonie Browne, Gen. *eodem* ...	...	25
	Robert Brudnell, Gen. *eodem* ...	...	25
	George Sheffield, Gen. *eodem* ...	...	25
June.	Sir James Harrington, Knight, *secundo Junii*		100

SALOP.

			£.
March.	Robert Eyton 18 *die Marcii* ...	...	25
	Thomas Onslowe, Armiger 22 *die Marcii*	...	25
	Richard Prince 24 *die Marcii* ...	...	25
	William Fowler 26 *die Marcii* ..	...	25
	Charles Foxe, Arm. 20 *die Marcii*	...	100
Aprill.	Thomas Corbett *tercio die Aprilis*...	...	25
	Rowland Barker, of Hammond, Armiger	...	50
	Robert Irelande *quarto die Aprilis*	...	25
	Frauncis Gatrice 8 *die Aprilis* ...	...	30

		£.
Aprill.	Richard Lea *eodem*	30
	Andrew Chorlton *eodem...*	30
	Frauncis Kynnaston *eodem*	25
	Robert Powell *eodem*	25
	Robert Mooreton *eodem...*	25
	Edward Lutwich *eodem ...*	25
	Frauncis Newport *eodem*	50
	Richard Hopton *eodem ...*	25
	William Leighton *eodem*	30
	Jerom. Corbett *eodem*	30
	Richard Lloid *eodem*	25
	Edward Gifford *eodem ...*	25
	John Brooke *eodem*	30
	Richard Owen *eodem*	25
	Edward Corbett, of Longmore *eodem*	25
	Richard Cressett 11 *die Aprilis* ...	30
	Thomas Burton *eodem ...*	25
	Adam Lutley *eodem*	25
	Rowland Lacon, Arm. 13 *die Aprilis*	50
	Roger Kynnaston 14 *die Aprilis* ...	25
	Edward Walter *eodem ...*	25
	Thomas Myne 15 *die Aprilis*	25
	William Preene 18 *die Aprilis*	25
	Elizabeth Alkinton 19 *die Aprilis...*	25
	Thomas Lawley *eodem ...*	25
	Thomas Powell *eodem ...*	25
	Edward Davies 21 *die Aprilis*	25
	Robert Needeham, Arm. 27 *die Aprilis*	50
	Thomas Perrins *ultimo die Aprilis*	25
	Thomas Kymmarsley 27 *die Aprilis*	30
	William Phillips, of Craicton 24 *Aprilis*	25
Maye.	Frauncis Albanie *quinto die Maii...*	30
	William Hopton, Arm. 8 *die Maii*	30
	Thomas Williams, Arm. 13 *die Maii*	25
	Morrice Ludlowe, Gen. *eodem*	25
	Alice Corbett, of Stoke, Vidua *eodem*	50
	George Vernon, of Hodnet, Gen. *eodem*	25
October.	Richard Ketlesbie 13 *die Octobris* ..	25

£.

October. Robert Acton, of Aldenham   27 *die Octobris*...   30

Novemb. Humfrey Brigge   11 *die Novembris*   ...   30
Humfrey Hill   19 *Novembris*   50

SOMERSETT.

March. John Sydenham, of Leigh   22 *die Marcii*   50
Richard Watkins, of Hollwell   *eodem*   25
John Davyson, Gen.   25 *die Marcii*   25

Aprill. John Bushe, of Brodfeild   *primo die Aprilis*...   50
Robert Holworthie   *secundo die Aprilis*   ...   25
Richard Bidgood   *eodem*   25
Gyles Gilbert   *eodem*   50
Jane Smithe, of Longe Ashton   *quinto die Aprilis*   25
Joane Rodney   *eodem*   25
George Lutterell, Armig.   8 *die Aprilis*   ...   50
Thomas Dyer   *eodem*   25
John Pirrey, Gen.   *eodem*   25
Walter Hodges   *eodem*   25
Sir John Stawell, Miles   *eodem*   ...   100
Thomas Leigh, of Welles   *eodem* ...   25
Nicholas Wadham, Armig.   *eodem*...   50
John Harrys, of Otheric   *eodem*   25
Hugh Bampfeild, Armiger, of North Cadburic   *eodem*   100
John Windham, of Orchard   *eodem*   ...   25
Joane Windham, Vid.   *eodem*   25
Edward Bevill, of Wells   *eodem*   25
George Gilbert   *eodem*   25
George Tilly, Gen. of Pointingdon   *eodem*   25
Roberte Cuffe, Gen.   *eodem*   ...   25
John Farewell   *eodem*   50
John Frauncis, Ar.   *eodem*   ...   25
Edmonde Windham   *eodem*   ...   25
Robert Sommer, of Othery   9 *die Aprilis*   25
Mawde Smithe, Vid.   *eodem*   ...   25

			£.
Aprill.	Richarde Walton *eodem*		25
	John Pearham, Gen. of Adbearc *eodem* ...		25
	Thomas Carew, Gen. *eodem*		25
	Walter Weaver *eodem*		25
	William Reade *eodem*		25
	Robert Jennyngs 11 *die Aprilis*		25
	Elizabeth Simpson, Vid. *eodem*		25
	John Lye *eodem*		25
	John Harrington, Ar. *eodem*		50
	William Galhampton 14 *die Aprilis* ...		25
	Symon Saunders 15 *die Aprilis*		50
	George Upton, Armiger 17 *die Aprilis* ...		25
	William Hodges, Gen. *eodem*		25
	John Hodges, Gen. *eodem*		25
	William Cowx 11 *die Aprilis*		25
	William Welshe *eodem*		25
	Christofer Kenne, Armiger *eodem*... ...		50
	Thomas Coward, of Shepton Mallett *eodem* ...		25
	Thomas Hodges *eodem*		25
	Thomas Wale, of Yatton *eodem*		25
	Dorothie Morgan, Vidua *eodem*		25
	Robert Webb 26 *die Aprilis*		50
	Richard Yeetes *eodem*		25
	Sir Henrie Portman, Miles 9 *die Aprilis* ...		100
	Mathew Ewens, Armiger *eodem*		25
Maye.	William Symes, of Chard *tercio die Maii* ...		50
	John Every, of Broadwaie *eodem*		25
	John Hawker 13 *die Maii*		25
	Thomas Raymond 17 *die Maii*		25
June.	Henric Keemer, Armiger 13 *die Junii* ...		50
	Joane Cutt, Vidua 7 *die Junii*		25
	John Afford, of Norton 6 *die Junii* ...		25
July.	———· Stewkeley, Vidua *ultimo die Julii*		25
October.	Roberte Hendley *the 4 of October*		50
	John Cogan *the 6 of October*		25
	John Uppall *the 7 of October*		25

		£.
October.	John Stephans *the* 30 *day*	25
	Baldwyn Deacon *the* 31 *day*	25
	John Welshave *the same day*	25
Decemb.	John Standerwicke *the first of December*	25
	Richard Mawdley *the* 6 *day*	25

STAFFORD.

		£.
March.	Thomas Leveson, Armiger 13 *die Marcii*	25
	Richard Brooke, Armiger *eodem*	25
	William Withall, Gen. *eodem*	25
	Roger Fowke, Gen. *eodem*	25
Aprill.	Edward Aston, Arm. *primo die Aprilis*	50
	John Chetwyn, Armiger *eodem*	25
	Raffe Snede, Armiger *eodem*	25
	Thomas Skrymsher, Gen. *eodem*	25
	Symon Biddall, Gen. *eodem*	25
	Richard Oteley, Gen. *eodem*	25
	Richard Flier, Gen. *eodem*	25
	Nicholas Blackwell, Gen. *eodem*	25
	James Skrymsher, Arm. *eodem*	25
	Walter Stanley, Arm. *eodem*	25
	Walter Heveningham, Arm. *eodem*	25
	Walter Fowler, Armiger *eodem*	25
	John Collman, Gen. *eodem*	25
	Edward Litleton, Arm. *eodem*	25
	Thomas Parke, Gen. *eodem*	25
	Phillip Okeover, Armiger *eodem*	25
	Frauncis Biddull, Armiger *eodem* ..	25
	William Crompton, Armiger	25
	Oliver Richardson, Gen. *eodem*	25
	Richard Smithe, Gen. *eodem*	25
	Dame Marie Leveson, Vid. *sexto die Aprilis*...	25
	Raffe Thickins, Gen. *eodem*	25
	Sir Raffe Egerton, Miles *eodem*	25
	Edward Noble, Gen. *eodem*	25

£.

Aprill.	William Comberford, Gen. *eodem* ...	...	25
	Raffe Egerton, Armiger *eodem*	...	...	25
	William Botton *eodem* ...	..	....	25
	Thomas Bowyer, Gen. *eodem*	...	...	25
	James Weston, Gen. 13 *die Aprilis*	...	25
	William Bowyer, Arm. *eodem*	...	...	25
	John Sheffington, Arm. *eodem*	...	...	25
	Richard Creswell, Gen. *eodem*	...	...	25
	Richard Bradshaw, Gen. *eodem*	...	...	25
	George Cradock, Mercer *eodem*	...	..	25
	John Wolridge, Gen. *eodem*	...	...	25
	Thomas Huntbach, Gen. *eodem*	...	...	25
	John Bardell, Gen. *eodem*	...	...	25
	Dame Alice Litleton, Vid. *eodem* ...	...	25
	John Mitton, Armiger *eodem*	...	...	25
	Edward Leigh, Armiger *eodem*	...	...	50
	John Wirley, Armiger *eodem*	...	...	25
	Richard Dorrington, Mercer *eodem*	...	25
	Robert Horwoode, *the* 12 *of April* ...	...	25

SUFFOLK.

£.

Apryll.	Jasper Sharpe *quinto die Aprilis* ...	...	25
	William Baker *eodem* ...	...	...	25
	Peter Kembold *eodem* ...	...	...	25
	Thomas Goodrich, Jun. ...	...	...	25
	John Revell *eodem* ...	...	...	25
	William Alman 7 *die Aprilis*	...	...	25
Aprill.	William Kilham 12 *die Aprilis* ...	...	25
Maye.	John Withers 14 *die Maii*	...	...	25
Aprill.	Henric Coppinger 28 *die Aprilis* ...	...	25
	Steven Ashewell, of Litle Saxham 19 *die Aprilis*	25
	George Smithe, of Forncham all Saints 26 *Aprilis*	25
	John Chenerie, of Exninge *eodem* ...	...	25

I

£

Aprill.	William Alston, of Newton 7 *Aprilis*	...	50
	Roger Marten, of Melford, Arm. 17 *Aprilis*	...	25
	Frauncis Maunocke, Arm. 24 *die Aprilis*	...	50
	John Brande, of Boxford 15 *die Aprilis*	...	50
	Widowe Daniell, of Acton 14 *die Aprilis*	...	25
	Widowe Drurie, of Lausell 10 *die Aprilis*	...	25
	John Winterfloud, of Assington 14 *Aprilis*	...	25
	Thomas Alston, of Edwardston 7 *Aprilis*	...	25
Aprill.	William Risbie, of Thorpe 19 *Aprilis*	...	25
Maye.	John Marten, of Bilston *secundo die Maii*	...	25
Aprill.	Edward Talkerne, of Witherfeild, Arm. 18 *Aprilis*	...	25
	William Fryar, of Clare 19 *Aprilis*	...	25
	Raphe Turner, of Stoke juxta Neyland 18 *Aprilis*	...	25
	Richard Kinge, of Stansfeild 14 *die Aprilis*	...	25
	John Rey, of Denston 16 *die Aprilis*	...	25
	John Smithe, of Hundon 7 *die Aprilis*	...	25
	Thomas Browne, of Hundon 18 *Aprilis*	...	25
	John Killingworth, of Bradley Magna 14 *Aprilis*		25
	John Warren, of Bradley Magna *eodem*	...	25
	William Devenet, of Poslingford 18 *die Aprilis*		25
	John Masham, of Badwell 28 *die Aprilis*	..	25
	Robert Hovell, alias Smithe, of Aishefeild 24 *Aprilis*	..	25
	George Nonne, of Weston 14 *Aprilis*	...	25
	Bartholmew Cotton, of Barneham 11 *die Aprilis*		25
	John Norton, of Ixworth 22 *die Aprilis*	...	25
	John Thurston, of Hoxon, Arm. *eodem*	...	25
	Lambert Nollorth, of Kelshall 15 *die Aprilis*		25
	Thomas Neeche, of Mendham *eodem*	...	25
	John Blewbold, of Mendham 18 *die Aprilis*	...	25
	Nicholas Barber, of Tresingfeild 7 *die Aprilis*		25
	Henrie Kinge, of Brundishe 21 *die Aprilis*	...	25
	Widowe Nicholls, of Laxfeild *eodem*	..	25
	Robert Barrett, of Laxfeild *eodem*	...	25
	Symon Cooke, of Laxfeild *eodem*	...	25

Aprill.	Thomas Fuller, of Tannyngton 22 *die Aprilis*	25
	William Dade, of Tannyngton 28 *Aprilis* ...	25
	Nicholas Lingwood, of Baddingham 21 *Aprilis*	25
	Reignold Morgan, of Soham 24 *die Aprilis* ...	25
	James Grudgefeild, of Stradbrooke 21 *die Aprilis*	25
	George Downinge, of St. Aldies 23 *Aprilis* ...	25
	William Gowche, of St. Margaretts *eodem* ...	25
	Richard Porter, of St. Nicholas 21 *die Aprilis*	25
	William Sydner, of Blundston, Arm. 25 *Aprilis*	25
	Roger Hullock, of Gislam 18 *Aprilis* ...	25
	James Sellinge, of Carleton *eodem* ...	25
	Humfrey Brewster, of Wrentham 24 *Aprilis*	25
	Edward Cooke, of Huntingfeild, Arm. 14 *Aprilis*	25
	Anne Bedingfeild, of Huntingfeild *eodem* ...	25
	William Miclewood, of Dunwiche 28 *die Aprilis*	25
	John Smithe, of Crackfeild 23 *die Aprilis* ...	25
	Anthonie Bull, of Sprawton *quarto die Aprilis*	25
	Thomas Goddinge, of Frieston 21 *die Aprilis*	25
	Roberte Salmon, of Needham 25 *die Aprilis*	25
	William Style, of Gesbacke 21 *die Aprilis* ...	25
	William Blomefeild, of Aspelstonham *eodem*	25
	Barnabie Gibson, of Litle Stenham *eodem* ...	25
	Richard Shepperd, of Mickfield *eodem* ...	25
	Henrie Gilbert, of Fynborough 9 *Aprilis* ...	25
	Edward Sulyard, of Wetherden 19 *Apnilis* ...	50
	William Prettiman, of Bawcton 21 *Aprilis* ...	50
	———·——— Golding, Vidua, of Eye 22 *Aprilis*	25
	Myles Docker, of Mendlesham 24 *Aprilis* ...	25
	Frauncis Sherman, of Brewesworth 19 *Aprilis*	25
	Roger Graye, of Frauson 9 *Aprilis* ...	25
	William Spurdance, of Fraunson 14 *Aprilis*	25
	John Oswood, of Gylington 28 *die Aprilis* ...	25
	Thomas Pretiman, of Bawcton *eodem* ...	25
	Thomas Rivett, of Brocford 24 *Aprilis* ...	25
	Frauncis Colbye, of Glenham Parva, Armiger 16 *Aprilis*	25
	Richard Brooke, of Norton *eodem*... ...	25
	Thomas Bennet, of Trimley 21 *die Aprilis* ...	25
	Geffrie Armiger, of Aishe *eodem*	25

		£.
Aprill.	Thomas Fostall, of Pettaugh 25 *Aprilis* ...	25
	John Tiler, of Framsden 24 *Aprilis* ...	25
	George Harrison, of Debenham *eodem* ...	25
	Thomas Mather, of Sutton 26 *Aprilis* ...	25
	William Burwell, of Sutton 26 *Aprilis* ...	25
	Robert Dowe, of Dallinger *eodem*.. ...	25
	William Bull, of Bouldge *eodem*	25
	John Longe, of Lyvermere 29 *Aprilis* ...	25
Maye.	Robert Webb, of Freckenham *quinto die Maii*	25
	Widowe Burrage, of Lackford *sexto die Maii*	25
	Thomas Mawltnard, of Downham	25
	Robert Kerrington, of Reade 24 *die Maii* ...	25
	——— Barker, Vidua, of Neyland, *primo die Maii*	25
	Andrew Kyme, of Elmesett 25 *Maii* ...	25
	Thomas Wilson, of Clare 16 *die Maii* ...	25
	Thomas Rowninge, of Hunden *quinto die Maii*	25
	Edward Rookewood, of Ewston, Armiger 8 *die Maii*	50
	William Harrison, of Walsham *quinto die Maii*	25
	William Derow, of Baddingham *sexto die Maii*	25
	Margarett Armiger, of Southold *quinto die Maii*	25
	Roberte Launce, of Metfcild 25 *die Maii* ...	25
	John Reade, of Weston, Arm. *tercio die Maii*	50
	Thomas Farneyle, of Westcreting 13 *die Maii*	25
	Hugh Joanes, of Gipping 21 *die Maii* ...	25
	Sir Thomas Cornewallis, Miles *secundo die Maii*	100
	Richarde Shorte, of Thornedon 12 *die Maii*...	25
	John Pennynge, of Eye *secundo die Maii* ...	25
	Thomas Smithe, of Wiverston *quinto die Maii*	25
	Robert Hall, of Palgrave 22 *die Maii* ...	25
	The Ladie Vicount Hereford 27 *die Maii* ...	50
	James Coe, of Orford *quinto die Maii* ...	25
	Nicholas Edgar, of Glemham Magna 8 *die Maii*	25
	Thomas Squire, of Alborough 13 *die Maii* ...	25
	Edmonde Mathew, of Claxton *primo die Maii*	25
	John Finche, of Tuddennam *eodem* ...	25
	Michaell Lancaster, of Walton 7 *die Maii* ...	25
	John Glover, of Ayshe *secundo die Maii* ...	25
	Arthur Pennynge, of Kettleborough *eodem* ...	50

		£.
Maye.	William Pitman, of Woodbridge *secundo die Maii*	25
	Anthonie Flicke, of Kettleborough 26 *die Maii*	25
	John Barker, of Ipswich *tercio die Maii* ...	50
	Nicholas Bedinfeild, of Gislingham 18 *Maii*...	25
June.	Michaell Hare, of Bruseyard, Arm. 9 *Junii*	50
	John Prettie, of Denham 11 *die Junii* ...	25
	Thomas Tymperley, of Hintlesham, *quinto die Junii*	25
July.	William Harper, Sen, of Wingfeild *secundo die Julii*	50

SURREY.

		£.
Feb.	William Sugden, of Newington 19 *die Februarii*	25
	Sisley Fletcher, of St. Olives, Vid. 24 *die Februarii*	25
	Thomas Shawe, of Worplesdon *eodem* ...	25
	John Carrill, of Wonnershe, Gen. 26 *die Februarii*	25
	James Shawe, of Guildeford, Clothier *eodem*	25
	John Paine, of Barmondsey, Gen. *eodem* ...	25
	Robert Brodbridge, of Guildford, Clothier *eodem*	25
	Roberte Forthe, Master of the Chauncerie *eodem*	50
	Sir Nicholas Woodroffe, Miles 27 *die Februarii*	50
	Helen Harrison, of St. Olives, Vidua *eodem*...	25
March.	William Haines, of Newington, Gen. *primo die Marcii*	25
	Frauncis Browne, of Ayshe, Ar. *secundo die Marcii*	25
	Mathew Lake, of Marten, Gen. *tercio die Marcii*	25
	William Lambold, of Woking *quarto die Marcii*	25
	Walter Newdigate, of Newdigate *quinto Marcii*	25
	William Atlee, of East Clandon *eodem* ...	25
	John Constable, of Newdigate *eodem* ...	25

		£.
March.	Thomas Rogers, of Wisley *eodem*	25
	Bartholomew Clark, Deane of th'arch'es 6 *Marcii*	50
	John Derrick, of Guildford, Sen. 7 *die Marcii*	25
	Sir Henrie Weston, Miles 11 *die Marcii* ...	100
	Thomas Brende, Gen. 14 *die Marcii* ...	50
	William Wignoll, of Tanridge, Merchant 15 *Murcii*	50
	Margeret Saunders, Vid. *eodem*	25
	William Heather, of Dorkinge 17 *die Marcii*	25
	Jo. Emersam, of St. Salviors, Draper 19 *die Marcii*	25
	Dame Julian Holcroft, of Stretham, Vid. 21 *Marcii*	50
	Edward Heath, of Clapham, Gen. 22 *die Marcii*	25
	Thomas Edward, of Ewhurst *eodem* ...	25
	John Woorsopp, of Clapham, Gen. *eodem* ...	25
	Robert Livesey, Armiger 25 *die Marcii* ...	50
	Henrie Hayward, Fishmonger 28 *die Marcii*	100
Apryll.	Richard Hill, of Shere, Gen. 17 *die Aprilis* ...	25
	Richard Sawyer, of Abingworth 23 *Aprilis* ...	25
	John Lee, of Abingworth 14 *die Aprilis* ...	25
	Christofer Crust, of Lee *eodem*	25
	Anne Cure, of Southwarke, Vid. 22 *Aprilis* ...	50
	William Myll, Armiger, Clerke of the 24 *Aprilis*	50
	John Carpenter, of Westbarnes 24 *Aprilis* ...	25
	Myles Wilkenson, of St. Salviors, Baker 26 *Aprilis*	25
	Beatrice Gresham, of Titsey, Vidua 28 *Aprilis*	50
Maye.	William Gardiner, Arm. 8 *die Maii* ...	50
	Richard Yeomans, of Waddenn 30 *Maii* ...	25
	Roberte Faire, of St. Marie Overies *eodem* ...	25
	John Cowper, of Capell, Arm. *eodem* ...	25
October.	William Evans, of Southwarke, Merchant Tailor 25 *Oct.*	25
	Bryan Pattison, of Southwarke, Vintener *eodem*	25
	John Pigeon, of Southwarke, Grocer 22 *Octobris*	25

SUSSEX.

		£.
March.	Henrie Goringe *secundo die Marcii*	100
	George Goring *quinto die Marcii*	100
	Edward Gage *eodem*	60
	John Eversfeild 7 *die Marcii*	100
	John Damrell 10 *die Marcii*	25
	Edward Goodwin 19 *die Marcii*	50
	Edward Paine, Jun. *eodem*	25
	William Holland *eodem*...	100
	John Farrington *eodem*	25
	Walter Edmondes 21 *die Marcii*	40
	Thomas Bowyer 26 *die Marcii*	30
	Thomas Michell *eodem*	50
	Thomas Greene *eodem*	25
	Thomas Bourde *ultimo die Marcii* ...	30
	John Watersfeild *eodem*... ...	30
Aprill.	John Shelley *primo die Aprilis*	40
	William Bartelott *eodem*	25
	William Aylewyne *eodem*	40
	Thomas Peirse *eodem*	40
	Edward Covett *secundo die Aprilis* ...	30
	Thomas Luxford *eodem*	30
	Robert Whitfeild *eodem*...	100
	John Stidman 7 *die Aprilis*	25
	Robert Whitpaine *eodem*	60
	Edward Luxford *eodem* ..:	25
	William Coldman *eodem*	25
	Edward Grey *eodem*	25
	John Awman 10 *die Aprilis*	50
	John Whetley *eodem*	30
	Dorothie Lewknor *eodem*	40
	John Rose *eodem*	40
	Thomas Wyatt, Senior *eodem*	25
	Richard Cooke 11 *die Aprilis*	25
	Thomas Taylor, Senior *eodem*	25
	John Cowper *eodem*	30
	John Bynwyn *eodem*	25
	Thomas Betesworth *eodem*	30
	Peter Betesworth *eodem*...	50

					£.
Aprill.	Walter Double *eodem* ...	...	...		50
	Thomas Pelham *eodem* ...	...	...		30
	Jacob Plummer *eodem* ...	...	...		25
	William Newton *eodem* ...	...	...		25
	John Lynton *eodem* ...	...	...		25
	Ellice Smithe *eodem* ...	...	...		25
	Edward Maninge 12 *Aprilis*	...	...		25
	Thomas Cobden *eodem* ...	...	...		25
	Roberte Harison *eodem* ...	...	...		25
	John Baker *eodem* ...	...	...		25
	John Chambers 13 *Aprilis*	...	...		50
	John Cowper *eodem* ...	...	...		25
	Beniamyn Pellet *eodem* ...	...	...		25
	Robert Grey *eodem* ...	...	...		25
	Adam Rackton *eodem* ...	...	...		25
	Richard Earneley 15 *die Aprilis* ...	...			30
	Robert Younge *eodem* ...	...	...		30
	Thomas Christmas *eodem*	...	...		25
	Thomas Glyde 10 *die Aprilis*	...	...		40
	William Burdett *eodem* ...	...	...		25
	John Davey *eodem* ...	...	...		25
	John Dunton 20 *die Aprilis*	...	...		25
	John Carrill *eodem* ...	...	...		100
	Thomas Alfrey *eodem* ...	...	...		30
	Nicholas Fowle *eodem* ...	...	...		40
	Edward Elsicke *eodem* ...	...	...		25
	Thomas Sherley, Miles *eodem*	...	...		100
	Walter Covert *eodem* ...	...	...		100
	John Smith 21 *die Aprilis*	...	...		25
	Frauncis Garton *eodem* ...	...	...		30
	William Wintershall *eodem*	...	...		50
	Thomas Stilliaurde *eodem*	...	...		50
	William Morley *eodem* ...	...	...		60
	Anthonie Kempe *eodem* ...	...	...		100
	William Davie *eodem* ...	...	...		25
	John Fraie *eodem* ...	...	...		50
	Richard Iden *eodem* ...	...	...		25
	Edward Carrell 22 *die Aprilis*	...	...		100
	John Selwyn *eodem* ...	...	...		50
	Alexander Sheppard *eodem*	...	...		40

		£.
Aprill.	John Bynde *eodem*	25
	Richard Farnefold *eodem*	30
	Frauncis Challinor 23 *Aprilis*	40
	John Lover *eodem*	25
	Richard Leatch 24 *die Aprilis*	40
	John Levett *eodem*	40
	John Relf 25 *die Aprilis*	25
	George Maie *eodem*	50
	Edward Hawes *eodem*	30
	Anthonie Stapley 26 *die Aprilis*	40
	Thomas Pelham *eodem*	100
	Jacob Hobson 28 *die Aprilis*	40
	John Bullman *ultimo die Aprilis*	25
	William Alferey *eodem*	25
	John Howell *eodem*	25
Maye.	Edward Culpepper, Armiger *primo die Maii*	100
	Robert Vincent *eodem*	25
	Thomas Collins *sexto die Maii*	25
	John Leedes 7 *die Maii*...	100
	John Sherley 18 *die Maii*	30
	Richard Gefferey *eodem*	40
	John Freebodie *eodem*	25
August.	Thomas Comber 6 *die August*	25
	Richard Bellingham *eodem*	25
Septemb.	Robert Woulgar *primo die Septembris* ...	25
	George Greene 21 *die Septembris*	40
	Thomas Culpepper 25 *die Septembris* ...	30
October.	Richard Michelborne *tercio die Octobris* ...	100
	Ste. Borde 7 *die Octobris*	30
	Roger Gratewich 11 *die Octobris*	100

WARRWICK.

		£.
Feb.	William Broughton, of Lowford Armiger 20 *Februarii*	40
	Raphe Sheldon, of Weston, Armiger 15 *die Februarii*	50
March.	William Skynner, of Rowington, Gen. *quinto die Marcii*	25
	Anthonie Shuckborough, of Shuckborough, Armiger 7 *die Marcii*	} 25
	Richard Petifer, of Dorcett Magna 12 *die Marcii*	25
	Walter Leigh, of Radwaie *eodem*	25
	William Kinge, of Burmingham 14 *die Marcii*	25
	Mrs. Anne Peto, of Chesterton, Vidua 27 *die Marcii*	25
	William Peto, of the same, Gen. *eodem* ...	25
	Mrs. Margarett Knowlys, of Nuneton, Vidua 18 *die Marcii*	40
	Robert Wilcocks, of Brawne 19 *dieMarcii* ...	25
	Thomas Asheley, of Woolvey, Gen. *eodem* ...	25
	William Fetherston, of Packwood 21 *die Marcii*	25
	Thomas Leigh, of Stoule, Armiger 31 *die Marcii*	40
	Gabriell Powltney, of Knowle, Gen. *secundo die Marcii*	25
Aprill.	Richard Goodale, of Atherston 6 *die Aprilis*	25
	Dame Jane Deverux, of Merryvale, Vidua 11 *die*	25
	Samuell Marrowe, of Barkeswell, Armiger 21 *die*	50
	Rice Griffyne, of Broome Regis, Gen. 20 *die Aprilis*	25
Maye.	William Collmer, of Burmingham 10 *die Maii*	25
	John Warde, of the same *eodem*	25
	William Sudvile, of Edson, Gen. 12 *die Maii*	25
	John Edes, of Ashorne 22 *die Maii* ...	25
	Ambrose Willes, of Fenycompton *eodem* ...	25
	Humfrey Ferrers, of Tamworth, Armiger 28 *die*	40
June.	Barthol. Hales, of Snitterfeild, Gen. *quarto Junii*	25
	Thomas Underhill, of Etington, Gen. 7 *die Junii*	25

		£.
June.	Nicholas Lane, of Bridgtowne *eodem* ...	25
	Richard Midlemore, of Edgbaston, Armiger 9 *die Junii* ...	25
	Andrew Archer, of Tamworth, Gen. *eodem* ...	25
	William Pendleburie, of Witchford 11 *die Junii*	12
	Edward Deverux, of Castle Bromage, Armiger 26 *die Junii* ...	25
July.	Richard Corbett, of Meryden, Armiger *quinto die Julii* ...	25
	Thomas Repington, of Armington, Gen. 21 *die*	25
	Richard Barker, Alderman 15 *die Julii* ...	25
	Edward Burrowes, Alderman *eodem* ...	25
	Henrie Briers, Alderman *eodem* ...	25
	John Rogerson, Draper *eodem* ...	25
	John Ryle *eodem* ...	25
August.	Thomas Throckmerton, of Coughton, Armiger *quinto die Augusti*	} 50

WILTES.

		£.
March.	John Thistlethaite *the 8 of March* ...	25
	Sir Walter Hungerford *the 10 of March* ...	50
	Edward Hungerford *the same day* ...	25
	Edward Horton *the same day* ...	50
	John Longe, Sen. *the 14 of March* ...	25
	Roger Blagden *the same day* ...	25
	Edward Longe *the 15 of March* ...	25
	John Truslowe *the 16 of March* ...	25
	Thomas Goddard *the 17 of March* ...	25
	Thomas Hulbert *the 18 of March* ...	25
	William Reade *the 19 of March* ...	25
	Charles Vaughan *the 21 of March* ...	25
	William Feltham *the same daye* ...	25
	John Dauntsey *the 31 of March* ...	25

£

April.	Lawrence Huyde	*the first of Aprill*	...	25
	William Cordrey	*the same day* ...	...	25
	Anthony Hynton	*the third day of Aprill*	...	25
	Michaell Erneley	*the same daye* ...	...	25
	Thomas Hutchins	*the same daye* ...	...	25
	Thomas Stevens	*the 5 of Aprill* ...	...	25
	Henry Longe	*the same day* ...	...	25
	Jone Mountpesson, Vidua	*the 6 of Aprill*	...	25
	John Flower	*the 7 day* ...	...	25
	Jefferey Whiteacre	*the 8 day*	...	25
	Thomas Dowse	*the same day*	...	25
	Fraunces Greene	*the same day*	..	25
	Stephen Duckett	*the same day*	...	25
	George Scrope	*the same day*	...	25
	Thomas Chaffyn	*the same day*	...	25
	William Pinckney	*the same day* ...	...	25
	William Eyre	*the same daye*	...	25
	William Webbe	*the same daye* ...	...	25
	Walter Hungerford	*the 9 of Aprill*	...	25
	William Sadler	*the 10 of Aprill* ...	...	25
	Thomas Lodge	*the same day* ...	...	25
	Nicholas St. John	*the 11 of Aprill*	...	25
	Bartholomewe Horsey	*the same day*	...	25
	William Baskervile	*the 13 of Aprill*	...	25
	William Jordan	*the same day* ...	...	25
	Thomas Toppe	*the same day* ...	...	25
	Thomas Bennett	*the 14 of Aprill* ...	...	25
	Thomazine Grove, Vidua	*the same day*	...	25
	William Young	*the 15 of Aprill* ...	...	25
	Anthony Disson	*the same daye* ...	...	25
	William Kemble	*the same daie* ...	...	25
	John Lovell	*the same daye* ...	...	25
	William Stamford	*the 16 of Aprill*	...	25
	John Hunte	*the 22 of Aprill* ...	...	50
	John Baylie	*the 24 of Aprill* ...	...	25
	Thomas Ivye	*the 25 of Aprill* ...	...	25
	William Button	*the 26 of Aprill* ...	...	25
	William Reeve, *the same daye*	...	...	25
	Richard Barnard	*the 29 of Aprill* ...	...	25
	John Thynne	*the 30 of Aprill* ...	...	25

		£.
Maye.	Richard Modie *the first of Maye* ...	25
	Alice Gawen, Vidua *the third of Maye*	25
	Edmunde Ludlowe *the 7 of Maye*...	25
	John Cornall *the 10 of Maye*	25
	Sir Edward Baynton *the 11 of Maye*	25
	Thomas Wallye *the 12 of Maye* ...	25
	Dame Jane Bridges *the 19 of Maye*	25
	Henrye White *the 25 of Maye* ...	25
	Anthony Geeringe *the 14 of Maye*	25
	William Lea *the 25 of Maye*	25
June.	Thomas Walton *the 4 of June*	25
	Nicholas Downe *the 8 of June*	25
	William Darrell *the 12 of June*	50
	Peter Polden *the 14 of June*	25
	William Noyes *the 15 of June*	25
	Richard Lavington *the same daye*...	25
	John Streete *the 15 of June*	25
	George Farewell *the 22 of June* ...	25
Julye.	Sir John Danvers *the first of Julye*	50
Novemb.	John Harding *the 12 of November*	25
	William Brouncker *the same daie* ...	25

WIGORNIA.

		£.
March.	William Gower, of Redmerley, Gen. 22 *die Marcii*	25
	Humfrey Pakington, of Chaddesley, Armiger 7 *die Marcii*	25
	Richard Greves, of Kingesnorton, Gen. 22 *die Marcii*	25
	William Whorewood, of Wedrockhill, Armiger *eodem*	25
	Richard Banaby, of Bocleton, Armiger *eodem*	25

		£.
March.	Richard Borne, of Ombresley *eodem* ...	25
	John Woorfeild, of Powicke *eodem* ...	25
Aprill.	John Washeborne, of Wicheford, Armiger 8 28 *die Aprilis*	25
May.	William Savadge, of Muchmalverne, Armiger *die Maii*	} 25
Aprill.	Walter Blount, of Sillington, Esq. *the 8th daie Aprill*	25
	Richard Gardiner, of Humbleton 19 *die Aprilis*	25
	Edward Pitt, of Kyne, Arm. 20 *die Aprilis*...	25
	Sir John Litleton, of Francklyn, Miles 30 *Aprilis*	100
	Edward Blounte, of Kitherminster, Arm. 27 *Aprilis*	25
	George Darbye, of Feckenham 28 *die Aprilis*	25
	Thomas Folliot, of Pirton, Armiger 19 *die Aprilis*	25
	William Fortescue, of Inckebarrowe, Armiger 27 *Aprilis*	25
	John Edgeock, of Edgeock, Gen. *eodem* ...	25
	Agnes Daston, of Elmeley Castle, Vidua 8 *Aprilis*	25
Maye.	John Smithe, of Ripple *tercio die Maii* ...	25
	Arthur Salwaie, of Stanford, Arm. 6 *die Maii*	25
	William Jeffries, of Home Castle, Gen. *tercio die Maii*	25
	John Talbott, of Grafton, Arm. 6 *die Maii* ...	50
	Henrie Cookes, of Shiltwood, Gen. *primo die Maii*	25
	John Rouse, of Rouselench, Arm. 27 *die Maii*	25
	Frauncis Walshe, of Sheldisloye, Arm. 4 *die Maii*	25
	John Withe, of Doritwich, Gen. *die Maii* ...	25
	The Baylieffe of the Cittie of Worcester 27 *die Maii*	200

		£.
June.	Raffe Woodward, of Alchurche 14 *die Junii*	25
October.	Hourie Dyneley, Arm. 11 *die Octobris* ...	25
	John Witherston, of Longdon *eodem* ...	25
	Hugh Lynton *eodem*	25
	George Shipside *eodem*	25
	Fraunces Russell *eodem*...	25
	Raffe Lencho *eodem*	25
	Edmonde Botho *eodem*	25
	Frauncis Clare, Arm. 18 *die Octobris* ...	25
	Thomas Sponner *eodem*...	25
	Richard Winsemore, of Fladburie *eodem* ...	25

YORKSHIRE.

		£.
Aprill.	William Copley *the* 30 *of Aprill*	25
	Robert Lewes *the same daye*	25
Maye.	John Savill *the first of Maye*	50
	Sir Christofer Hilliard *the second of Maye* ...	25
	John Genkyns *the same day*	50
	Roberte Sothebie *the same daye*	25
	Richard Horsfall *the* 5 *of Maye*	25
	Gervase Ayre *the* 13 *of Maye*	25
	George Twisfelloton *the same daye* ...	25
	Thomas Millner *the same daie*	25
	Brian Askewith *the same daie*	50
	William Parker *the same daie*	25
	Raphe Hunsbie *the* 14 *of Maye*	50
	Anthony Jackson *the same daie*	25
	Hugh Francklande *the same day*	50
	William Hungate *the same daye*	50
	Edward Rolston *the same daie*	25
	William Bates *the same daie*	50
	Katherine Radcliffe *the same daie*... ...	25
	Marmaduke Grymston *the* 15 *day*... ...	25
	William Oglethorpe *the same daie*... ...	25

				£.
Maye.	Roberte Trotter *the same daie* ...	...	...	25
	Roberte Rokeby *the 16 of Maie* ...	...	...	25
	George Tockletts *the 15 of Maie* ...	...	...	25
	John Sayer *the 16 daie* ...	...	...	100
	Richard Gascoinge *the same day* ...	...	...	50
	George Consett *the 17* ...	...	...	25
	John Armytage *the same day*	...	...	25
	John Constable *the same daie*	...	...	25
	Marmaduke Cholmeley *the same day*	...	...	25
	James Murtgaitroit *the 18*	...	...	25
	Richard Vaughan *the same daie* ...	...	...	25
	William Thorneton *the same daie* ...	...	...	50
	William Plompton *the 20*	...	...	30
	Christofer Blande *the same daie* ...	...	...	25
	William Nesse *the same daie*	...	...	25
	James Hebletwait *the same daie* ...	...	...	25
	John Milborne *the same daie*	...	...	50
	Frauncis Metham *the same daie* ...	...	...	50
	Thomas Gower *the same daie*	...	...	25
	Brian Crowther *the 21 of Maye* ...	...	...	25
	Richard Wadesworth *the same daie*	...	...	25
	Thomas Beresbie *the same daie* ...	...	...	25
	Raphe Salvyn *the same daie*	...	...	25
	Richard Darley *the same daie*	...	...	25
	Thomas Morelyffe *the same daie* ...	...	...	50
	Christofer Wandesford *the same daie*	...	...	25
	Raphe Lawson *the same daie*	...	...	50
	Elizabeth Pudsey, Vidua *the same daie*	...	...	30
	George St. Quintayne *the 22 of Maye*	...	...	25
	John Harryson *the same daie*	...	...	25
	Richard Vincent *the same daie*	...	...	25
	Richard Gascoigne *the same daie* ...	...	...	25
	John Ellys *the same daie*	...	...	25
	John Vavisor *the same daie*	...	...	25
	George Frith *the same daie*	...	...	25
	Richard Cowper *the same daie*	...	...	25
	William Wivell *the same daie*	...	...	25
	John Thorneholme *the 13 of May* ...	...	...	25
	Humfrey Burleston *the same daie* ...	...	...	25
	Thomas Southebie *the same daie* ...	...	...	25

			£.
Maye.	Robert Killingbeck *the same daie* ...	...	25
	John Hopton *the same daie* ...	...	25
	Walter Calverley *the same daie* ...	...	25
	George Holtbie *the same daie* ...	...	25
	William Horseley *the same daie* ...	...	25
	Henry Scrope *the same daie* ...	...	25
	Thomas Worral *the 25 of May* ...	...	25
	Reginald Heybar *the same daie* ...	...	25
	William Hartley *the same daie* ...	...	25
	Thomas Franck *the same daie* ...	...	30
	Thomas Conyers *the same daie* ...	...	25
	Richard Williams *the same daie* ...	...	25
	John Hausbie *the same daie* ...	...	25
	James Straingwayes *the same daie* ...	...	25
	John Craicroft *the 26 of Maye* ...	...	25
	William Strickland *the same daie* ...	...	25
	William Lawson *the same daie* ...	...	25
	Cyrill Arthington *the sam daie* ...	...	25
	Robert Oglethorpe *the same daie* ...	...	25
	John Romesden *the same daie* ...	...	100
	John Freiston *the 28 of Maie* ...	...	100
	William Addams *the same daie* ...	...	40
	Robert Wyvell *the same daie* ...	...	25
	Robert Wright *the 29 of Maie* ...	...	25
	John Lacye *the same daie* ...	...	25
	Fraunces Ratcliffe *the same daie* ...	...	25
	Christofer Consett *the 30 of May* ...	...	52
	John Dyneley *the same daie* ...	...	25
June.	Richard Foster *the second of June*	...	25
	Christofer Walham *the same daie* ...	...	25
	Richard Sunderland *the same daie*	...	25
	Gilbert Salltonstall *the same daie* ...	...	25
	William Fletcher *the same daie* ...	...	25
	Sir Thomas Danbye *the same daie*	...	50
	Leonarde Conyers *the same daie* ...	...	25
	Christofer Conyers *the 4 of June* ...	...	100
	George Savill *the 8 of June* ...	...	100
	Hyllary Daykins *the 12 of June* ...	...	25
	William Oglethorpe *the same daie* ...	...	50

L

			£.
June.	Walter Hawkesworth *the 18 of June*	...	25
	John Inglebie *the 21 of June* ... ·	...	50
	William Middleton *the 28 of June*...	...	25
	John Lacye *the same daie* ...	...	25
Julye.	James Sigiswicke *the 4 of Julye* ...	...	25
	Raphe Tankard *the 5 of Julie* ...	...	25
	Thomas Stevenson *the 17 of Julie*	...	25
	Marmaduke Langdall *the 26 of Julye*	...	50
	Thomas Whalley *the last of July* ...	...	·25
August.	Henrie Wythes *the first of August*..	...	25
	Richard Moone *the 3 of August* ...	...	25
	Anthony Wytham *the 9th of August*	...	25
Septemb.	Richard Ledgerd *the 3 of September*	...	25

F I N I S.

INDEX OF NAMES.

Cotherington, 23
Cotsford, 51
Cotton, 9, 22, 32, 58
Courson, 4
Courteney, 13
Cove, 15
Covert, 64
Covett, 63
Coward, 55
Cowerden, 35
Cowper, 8, 30, 42, 62, 63, 64, 72
Cowx, 55
Coxe, 22, 23 *twice*
Coxhall, 22
Cradock, 57
Craicroft, 73
Cranwell, 31
Crauford, 7
Crawley, 1, 2, 29
Crayford, 33
Cressett, 53
Creswell, 19, 57
Crew, 22 *twice*
Crispe, 47
Crofte, 27, 36
Crompton, 23, 41, 56
Cropley, 6, 20
Cropwell, 7
Croswell, 48
Crowther, 72
Crust, 62
Cubitt, 44
Cuffe, 54
Culpepper, 32, 65 *twice*
Cultheath, 34
Cure, 62
Curle, 26, 42
Curter, 6
Cutt, 24, 33, 35

DACOM, 17
Dade, 59
Dalby, 41
Dale, 11
Dalton, 8
Damrell, 63
Danbye, 73
Daniell, 30,
Dansey, 27
Danvers, 48, 69

Darby, 16, 70
Darley, 72
Darnell, 27
Darrell, 69
Daston, 70
Daunock, 45
Dauntsey, 67
Davenport, 9 *twice*
Davers, 3
Davie, 2, 6, 12, 13 *twice*, 45, 46,
    64 *twice*
Davies, 53
Davison, 38, 54
Dawbney, 2
Day, 7, 18, 42
Daykins, 73
Deacon, 56
Delves, 9
Denny, 45
Dennys 12, 22
Denton, 1
Denwoode, 33
Dermer, 29
Derrick, 62
Dethicke, 11 *twice*
Devenet 58
Deverell, 5
Deverux, 66, 67
Dewhurst, 35
Dey, 44
Diconson, 35
Digby, 36, 52
Dike, 33
Dinton, 2
Disson, 68
Derow, 60
Docker, 59
Doclon, 14
Doe, 3
Doles, 22
Donington, 3
Donnett, 32
Dormer, 4
Dorrington, 57
Double, 64
Dowe, 60
Downe, 69
Downes, 43
Downinge, 41, 51
Dowse, 68
Draper, 30, 38

Folkes, 6
Folliambe, 11
Folliott, 70
Folnebye. 39
Foorde, 22
Fortescue, 14 *twice*, 70
Forthe, 61
Fostall, 60
Foster, 2, 5, 6, 29, 73
Fountaine, 4
Fowke, 56
Foule, 31, 64
Fowler, 22, 23, 40, 52, 56
Foxe, 52
Fraie, 64
Framyngham, 43
Franck, 73
Francklande, 71
Francklyn, 41
Frannces, 11, 33, 47
Frauncis, 54
Freake, 15
Freebodie, 65
Freeman, 47
Freiston, 73
French, 18
Fretchville, 11
Frevyle, 17
Friar, 20
Frigge, 23
Fryar, 58
Frye, 37
Fuller, 19, 42, 59
Furse, 14
Futter, 44

GADNEY, 38
Gage, 63
Gale, 13
Galhampton, 55
Gamage, 5
Gambling, 38
Gardiner, 29, 62, 70
Garnaunce, 22
Garnons, 27
Garnett, 29
Garrarde, 3
Garth, 40
Garton, 64

Gascoigne, 72 *twice*
Gassington, 43
Gatrice, 52
Gawdric, 38
Gawen, 69
Gaybon, 46
Gaywood, 19
Gell, 11
Geeringe, 69
Gefferey, 65
Gelstopp, 49
Gerrarde, 34
Gerves, 49
Gery, 7
Gibbe 28
Gibbon, 31
Gibson, 59
Gifford, 13, 53
Gilbert, 12, 54 *twice*, 59
Gill, 11
Girdeon, 8
Girlington, 39
Glanvile, 13
Glascock, 20 *twice*
Gleane, 44
Glover, 60
Glyde, 64
Goddard, 24, 25, 67
Goddinge, 59
Godfrey, 25, 30 *twice*, 33
Golde, 14
Golding, 20, 59
Goodale, 66
Goodman, 2
Goodrich, 57
Goodrick, 7, 38
Goodridge, 14
Goodwin, 63
Gookyn, 31
Goringe, 63 *twice*
Goston, 49
Gover, 14
Gough, 21. 51
Gowche, 59
Gower, 69, 72
Gowld, 17
Grantham, 37
Gratewich, 65
Grave, 29, 44
Graveley, 29
Gravnor, 8

M

Heskeith, 35
Heveringham, 56
Heward, 48
Hext, 10
Heybar, 73
Hicklyn, 47
Hicks, 45
Hid, 9
Hide, 3 *twice*
Higgs, 4
Hill, 23, 54, 62
Hilliard, 71
Hilton, 35
Hinde, 5
Hirne, 45
Hitch, 7
Hobbes, 3, 5
Hobby, 21
Hobson, 25, 39, 65
Hodges, 23, 54, 55 *thrice*
Hodgson, 17
Hodilowe, 6
Hodson, 24
Holcroft, 62
Holland, 34, 63
Hollis, 50
Holliwell, 7
Holtbie, 73
Holworthie, 54
Homerston, 8
Honnywood, 33
Hooper, 16
Hoore, 26
Hopkins, 41
Hopper, 19
Hopton, 53 *twice*, 73
Hore, 46
Horne, 46
Horseley, 73
Horsey, 68
Horsfall, 71
Horton, 11, 67
Horwoode, 57
Hoskins, 16
Houghton, 35 *twice*
Houlton, 45
Hovell, 45, 58
Howell, 65
Howsdon, 6
Howse, 5 *twice*
Howson, 33

Hubbard, 44
Hubberd, 43
Hudson, 46
Huffman, 33
Hughes, 47
Hulbert, 67
Hullock, 59
Humfrey, 3
Hungate, 71
Hungerford, 51, 67 *twice*, 68
Hunsbie, 71
Hunt, 12, 25 *twice*, 52, 68
Huntbach, 57
Huntley, 22
Hurst, 13, 29
Husbonde, 46
Husse, 40
Hutchenson, 50
Hutchins, 3, 51, 68
Huyde, 68
Hyde, 29
Hynton, 68

IDEN, 64
Iley, 7
Inglebie, 74
Ingolsbie, 5
Irebye, 40
Ireland, 34 *twice*, 52
Isham, 47
Ive, 20
Ivye, 63

JACKMAN, 20, 26
Jackson, 71
Jakeman, 5
James, 43
Jamper, 25
Jeffries, 70
Jenkyns, 71
Jenkinson, 44, 47
Jennyngs, 4, 20, 55
Jennyson, 17
Jephson, 25
Jerningham, 45
Jessop, 50
Joanes, 60

PADGE, 25
   Page, 41
Pagett, 34
Pagrave, 43 *twice*
Paine, 61, 63
Pakington, 69
Palmer, 30, 49, 50
Palmes, 52
Paramor, 36
Pargitor, 47
Parke, 46, 56
Parker, 11, 71
Parkins, 3
Parkinson, 24
Parratt, 1
Parsons, 28, 50
Partridge, 22, 23
Pascow, 10
Paston, 43 *thrice*
Pate, 36
Patrick, 39
Pattison, 62
Payne, 2
Payton, 33
Peake, 25
Pearham, 55
Peach, 7
Peacock, 42
Peck, 7 *twice*, 44
Pedley, 30
Peirse, 63
Pelham, 4, 64, 65
Pell, 36, 38
Pellet, 64
Pendleburie, 67
Pendock, 50
Penny, 32
Penyuge, 60 *twice*
Penyston, 4
Perpointe, 37
Perrins, 53
Pescod, 26
Peter, 13 *twice*, 41
Peterson, 45
Petifer, 66
Peto, 66
Pettus, 45
Phage, 8
Phillipps, 13, 39, 53
Philpott, 26
Pickeringe, 47

Pie, 18, 44
Pierpointe, 49
Pigeon, 62
Pigott, 5, 60
Pike, 45
Pile, 25
Pilgryme, 7
Pinckney, 68
Pingell, 17
Pinke, 25
Pirrey, 23, 54
Pitman, 61
Pitt, 15, 70
Pittman, 24
Planner, 2
Pledall, 4
Pleydall, 3 *twice*
Plompton, 72
Ploomer, 33
Plott, 3
Plumbe, 37
Plummer, 64
Pocdage, 33
Pockington, 50
Pocock, 3
Pointz, 19, 21
Polden, 69
Poole, 9, 13, 24, 37
Pooles, 22
Pope, 25
Popple, 39
Porrye, 44
Porter, 11, 59
Potman, 31, 55
Potter, 19
Potts, 5
Poulton, 48
Povye, 42
Powlett, 18
Powltney, 66
Powell, 53 *twice*
Powndrell, 12
Prane, 3
Pratt, 6, 7, 44, 47
Preene, 53
Pregnish, 26
Prentice, 45
Preston, 30, 35 *twice*
Prettie, 61
Prettiman, 59 *twice*
Prideaux, 10, 13

Sawyer, 51, 62
Sayer, 19, 72
Scaresbeck, 34
Sclater, 11
Scorye, 41
Scott, 32
Scovell, 17
Scrope, 68, 73
Sea, 32
Seaman, 6
Searle, 19, 24, 26
Secker, 45
Sellinge, 59
Selwyn, 22, 24, 64
Sendie, 24
Serche, 28
Serger, 16
Seymour, 3, 16
Shadforth, 39
Shakerley, 9
Shallcrosse, 11
Sharpe, 32, 57
Shawe, 61 *twice*
Sheffe, 32
Sheffield, 52
Sheffington, 57
Sheldon, 13, 66
Shelley, 63
Sheppard, 64
Shepperd, 51, 59
Sheard, 36
Sherewood, 4
Sheriffe, 50
Sheringe, 45
Sherley, 47, 64, 65
Sherman, 15, 59
Sherwood, 28
Shipside, 71
Shorte, 60
Shuckborough, 66
Shugborow, 47
Shuttleworth, 35
Sidenham, 21
Sidley, 31, 32
Sidwaie, 16
Sigiswicke, 74
Silliard, 33
Simpson, 55
Singleton, 22, 35
Sitwell, 11
Skawen, 10
Skeale, 19
Skearne, 39

Skelton, 18
Skerne, 16
Skevington, 18
Skipwith, 39
Skootred, 8
Skroggs, 2
Skrymsher, 56 *twice*
Skymer, 14, 28, 66
Slade, 4
Smaleman, 27
Smith, 2, 3, 4, 6, 9, 10, 12, 14, 20,
22, 27, 30, 32, 36, 37, 40 *twice*,
45, 51, 52, 54 *twice*, 56, 57, 58,
59, 60, 64 *twice*, 70
Snede, 56
Snell, 7
Sommer, 54
Somner, 20 *twice*
Sorrell, 19
Sothebie, 71
South, 37
Southcott, 13
Southbie, 3, 72
Southland, 34
Southworth, 35
Spealte, 14
Specott, 13
Spencer, 12, 29
Sperke, 12
Spicer, 1, 15
Spier, 50 *twice*
Sponer, 46
Sponner, 71
Spracklyn, 33 *twice*
Spurdance, 59
Spurlinge, 29
Squire, 60
Srilles, 10
Stafford, 47
Stallen, 43
Stamford, 68
Standen, 40
Standeley, 9 *twice*
Standerwicke, 56
Standford, 73
Standishe, 19, 34, 35
Stanford, 36
Stanhopp, 48
Stanley, 39, 56
Staples, 18
Stapleton, 50
Stapley, 65
Staunton, 4, 50

N

Tresham, 41, 47
Trotter, 72
Trotman, 21, 24 *twice*
Trobridge, 13
Trowghton, 5
Truslowe, 67
Trust, 47
Tulfe, 26
Turbervile, 16
Turner, 20, 28, 58
Turvile, 36
Tutchett, 8
Twine, 24
Twisfelloton, 71
Tylney, 43
Tymperley, 61

UNDERHILL, 66
    Upcrofte, 46
Uppall, 55
Upton, 15, 55
Urry, 26
Uvedall, 15

VAUGHAN, 41 *twice*, 67, 72
    Vavisor, 72
Venables, 9, 26
Veime, 22
Vernon, 9, 18, 53
Vincent, 65, 72

WADE, 5, 7
    Wadesworth, 72
Wadham, 54
Wake, 48
Walcott, 40
Waldgrave, 46
Waldron, 13
Wale, 55
Walham, 73
Walker, 12, 19, 32, 36, 49
Wall, 19
Wallye, 69
Walmesly, 35 *twice*
Walronde, 37, 41

Walshe, 70
Walter, 53
Walton, 55, 69
Wandesford, 72
Warburton, 8, 9
Warde, 7, 31, 66
Warkeman, 23
Warne, 22
Warner, 44, 51
Warren, 29, 41, 58
Warrham, 31
Washbourne, 27, 70
Watersfeild, 63
Watkins, 54
Watson, 26, 47
Watton, 31
Watts, 16, 45
Weaver, 27 *twice*, 55
Webb, 4, 15, 22, 27, 55, 60
Weedon, 5
Welbury, 17
Welby, 39 *twice*
Welkshorne, 3
Wells, 31
Welshe, 12, 55
Welshave, 56
West, 5, 15
Westbie, 36
Weston, 57, 62
Wetherwick, 39
Whale, 7, 36, 44
Whalley, 46, 74
Whetcombe, 17
Whetley, 63
Whetnall, 32
Whichlowe, 4
Whipple, 44
White, 25 *thrice*, 69
Whiteacre, 68
Whitehead, 24
Whitfeild, 63
Whitinge, 22
Whitmore, 9, 50
Whitpaine, 63
Whittingham, 38
Whitton, 50
Whorewood, 69
Wiberd, 20
Wiett, 45
Wigley, 11
Wignoll, 62